W9-BUG-454

PRESENTED TO

Christine Blanchette
Angel # 1
With love & best wishes for a
speedy recovery —
De Colores —

BY

Paul & Dolores   April 15, 2003

INTO HIS ARMS

SIGMUND BROUWER

COUNTRYMAN

Copyright 1999 by Sigmund Brouwer

Published by J. Countryman,
a division of Thomas Nelson Inc., Nashville, Tennessee 37214

Project Editor—Terri Gibbs

All rights reserved. No portion of this publication may be reproduced, stored in
a retrieval system or transmitted in any form by any means—electronic,
mechanical, photocopying, recording, or any other—except for brief quotations
in printed reviews, without the prior written permission of the publisher.

All Scripture quotations in this book are from the New King James Version of
the Bible (NKJV), copyright© 1979, 1980, 1982, by Thomas Nelson, Publishers,
Inc. and are used by permission.

J. Countryman is a registered trademark of Thomas Nelson, Inc.

A J. Countryman Book

Designed by Koechel Peterson and Associates, Inc., Minneapolis, Minnesota

Front cover illustration by C. Michael Dudash. Art on pages 124–125 used with
permission from Bob Jones University Museum & Gallery.

ISBN: 0-8499-5467-3

Printed and bound in Belgium

FOR
JACK & MARSHA
COUNTRYMAN

CONTENTS

PREFACE

During the time I spent working on this book, I looked at the surroundings and events of the Gospels through the eyes of great historians. It was a joy. These writers painted such clear pictures that I spent much more time daydreaming than writing. What would it be like, I wondered time and again, to be there beside Jesus? I wondered too, about the people he changed through his teachings and miracles. How did they feel after they met him? Where did they go? How were their lives changed after meeting this man of love? And what about the children who saw or met him? How were their lives affected?

The stories in this book result from those questions. As I molded these stories around the events of the Gospels, my goal was to remain true to Scripture and historical facts. I cannot claim, however, that these stories reflect the actual thoughts and actions of any characters placed in the Gospels. My hope, instead, is to give the reader the same sense of wonder that I found in trying to see Jesus through the eyes of children around him.

Thank you, Terri Gibbs, for your wisdom and encouragement and advice as editor; any shortcomings in our efforts to present the Gospel stories from a new perspective fall squarely on my shoulders.

To Jack and Marsha Countryman, let me say here that wherever you go, you touch lives with your vision of publishing, and much more importantly, with your love. Cindy and I have been blessed by your friendship. This book is dedicated to you.

And Cindy, I always lean on your own childlike innocence and joy and the music you place in my heart. Thank you.

SIGMUND BROUWER
January 1999

Mary, the Girl-Child

A child, soon to give birth to a child.

Now of the usual age of engagement, perhaps just fourteen years old, this child is Mary.

She is alone when the angel Gabriel visits her in Nazareth.

An angel! With a message she can hardly believe!

His departure leaves her alone to dwell on his words. Alone and struggling to comprehend what it will mean to be visited by the Holy Spirit. Alone and thinking through the implications of a baby in her womb before she is wedded.

 What goes through her mind? The glory of serving the most high God? Or fear of idle gossip when her belly begins to swell? Does she look ahead with joy to giving the world One whose kingdom will never end? Or does she dread what Joseph might do if he does not believe her story?

Who can she turn to? Who will listen without laughter and scorn? Who will give comfort and support during the months ahead?

She is only a girl. A child about to carry a child. And now, with the angel gone, she is completely alone . . . with her doubts.

But she remembers the angel's words. Remembers how he had spoken of her cousin—an older woman who will also give birth through a miracle of God. Mary wonders if she can open her heart to this woman.

So the girl, Mary, prepares to leave Nazareth to visit her kinswoman, Elizabeth.

Now Mary arose in those days and went into the hill country with haste, to a city of Judah, and entered the house of Zacharias and greeted Elizabeth. And it happened, when Elizabeth heard the greeting of Mary, that the babe leaped in her womb; and Elizabeth was filled with the Holy Spirit. Then she spoke out with a loud voice and said, "Blessed are you among women, and blessed is the fruit of your womb!"

LUKE 1:39-42

As Mary journeys through the hills of Judea, how can she not be afraid? With every step she takes, worry and doubt torment her. Will Elizabeth make time for her? Will Elizabeth have compassion for an unwed girl with child?

For Mary, this journey to Judea is not easy—not through the heat and dust . . . not when she fears every passing stranger . . . not when any turn in the road might lead to thieves waiting in ambush.

For Mary, alone and afraid, the journey mirrors the journey of her soul. The mountains are steep. The valleys are low. How weary she must be, with so far to go. So far to reach Elizabeth. So far until she gives birth . . . until God's promise is delivered.

Finally, Mary arrives at the doorstep of her cousin Elizabeth, weary and ready for the worst.

The door is opened. Elizabeth invites her inside. Mary gives a greeting, perhaps pausing to see if Elizabeth is too angry to be disturbed.

But there is no anger here. In fact, there is great happiness! The older woman blesses Mary in a loud, joyful voice.

Mary's secret is not a secret she must struggle to tell, for Elizabeth knows it in the very moment of greeting, and rejoices because of it. It is great and glorious news! Indeed, the unborn child within Elizabeth's womb leaps with joy to hear Mary's voice.

Later, for this young girl, Mary, there will be shepherds and singing hosts of angels. There will be water that turns to wine. Her son, the Messiah, will bring healing and freedom to people from all walks of life. And there will also be the heartbreak of the Cross.

But in this moment, with dear Elizabeth full of the joy of the Holy Spirit, Mary's simple faith, the faith of a trusting child, receives its first divine reward.

 Mary is touched with joy. She turns her joy into song—a hymn that will echo over the centuries, down through the ages of time . . . to bring us all joy.

MARY'S SONG

My soul magnifies the Lord,
And my spirit has rejoiced in God
   my Savior.
For He has regarded the lowly state
   of His maidservant;
For behold, henceforth all
   generations will call me blessed.
For He who is mighty has done
   great things for me,
And holy is His name.
And His mercy is on those who fear Him
From generation to generation.
He has shown strength with His arm;
He has scattered the proud in the
   imagination of their hearts.
He has put down the mighty from
   their thrones,
And exalted the lowly.
He has filled the hungry with good things,
And the rich He has sent away empty.
He has helped His servant Israel,
In remembrance of His mercy,
As He spoke to our fathers,
To Abraham and to his seed forever.

LUKE 1:46−55

THE OLD WOMAN'S TALE

WHAT KIND OF SAVIOR

In his wonderful book, *The Life and Times of Jesus the Messiah*, Alfred Edersheim points out the contrasts between the humanity of Jesus and his divinity.

Jesus was born to a poor, young, unknown woman—yet an angel announced his birth.

Laid in a manger—a heavenly host sang his welcome.

After facing hunger and temptation in the desert, angels ministered to him.

Jesus was baptized in submission to John the Baptist, and immediately a voice from Heaven proclaimed his favor with God.

As he was tortured in the public humiliation of crucifixion, the sky darkened and the earth quaked.

Through the Gospels, we truly see Jesus as both man and God.

They had no idea it would be their last morning together in the temple, the old woman and the small girl, as they made their way slowly through the Temple's North Gate toward the Court of Women. Ahead, the temple mount rose gloriously above them, supported by columns of marble and plated gold. The smoke of sacrifices drifted upward from the altar to a sky, cloudless and pale blue with early morning softness.

 Around them, solitary worshipers hurried forward, ignoring the affection and conversation of the two as they made steady progress. They continued in this way, finally reaching the shade beneath the colonnades that surrounded the Court of Women. The square in front of them was vast, big enough to hold more than 15,000 worshipers. This early, however, it was nearly empty—except for several old men in priestly robes at the far end of the square.

"Can you see it in your mind?" the old woman asked the little girl. Although they had reached their first destination and the old woman no longer needed support, she kept a hand lightly on the girl's shoulders.

Marianne smiled. Every day when they reached this point—where the thirteen trumpet–shaped boxes stood to receive vows and offerings—the old woman, Anna, said the same thing. And every day Marianne listened and did not reply. She was only seven, but already understood how important it was for the old woman to share her memories.

"She was a mother with her firstborn," Anna said, "just as you shall be one day. She had taken her son to the priest to be blessed."

The old woman frowned. The priests at the end of the court were walking directly toward her and the little girl. The sight of them reminded her of something else. "Of course, those thieves demanded their five shekels of the mother."

Little Marianne giggled. How she adored this old woman and her fierce spirit. At first, when Marianne's mother had instructed her to help the old widow because she was one of their tribe, Marianne had done so strictly from obedience. Now, these daily walks from the upper city to the temple with the old woman were the highlight of Marianne's day. Anna told tales of their tribe, the tribe of Asher, and how the women of that tribe were celebrated for their beauty and their fitness to be wedded to the king. Anna spoke of her long dead husband, and of true love, and how she had never once considered marrying again, and how Marianne with her long dark hair and beautiful white smile would one day meet a man to love with all her heart, just as Anna had done.

"Then," Anna said, continuing her familiar story for the little girl, "after presenting her firstborn to the priests, this young mother went for her purification. I'm sure your own mother has told you what is expected of women, and how difficult the men of religion make it for us to reach our Father God."

Marianne giggled again. Anna often made it very clear how she scorned the Pharisees and their rigid rules. It was the luxury of the aged, Anna explained, not to fear anything except the God of Israel.

Anna pointed at some nearby steps. "And after this young woman had completed all the necessary rituals and payments, it was there that I finally saw her . . . and her baby in the arms of an old man named Simeon."

Marianne smiled. It had happened only a few months ago, but Anna had retold the story time and again, not only to her but to anyone in the temple courts who would listen.

"Simeon had waited all those years for the redemption of Israel," Anna continued, excitement rising in her voice, "and he found it in this baby—a boy named Yeshua! The Holy Spirit moved me too, and as Simeon praised God, I approached the mother and her baby. At that very moment I—"

Anna hesitated as the approaching men stopped abruptly in front of her.

"We wish to speak with you," the lead man said. Marianne found him frightening. His hooked nose and dark eyes above a long beard gave him the face of an angry eagle.

"Speak then," Anna said, sensing Marianne's fear and holding her close.

"It is unsuitable for you to continue harassing worshipers with your fanciful tales and ridiculous prophecies. Unless you cease, the temple police will be instructed to remove you and prohibit your return."

Held tightly against the old woman, Marianne felt Anna tremble—from rage.

"It is because of men like you that I long for our Redeemer," Anna said, her weak voice rising and growing strong. "You have let the synagogue and its teachings replace the Temple and God's presence within. All that remains pure and free and pointing toward the Father of our people is the Temple itself, surrounded by the corruption of money changers and animal markets and thousands of priests who live well by cheating the poor. Not for those priests have I fasted and prayed here every day for over sixty years, but for God within the Temple. And now you dare deny me that?"

Now there was one, Anna, a prophetess, . . . a widow of about eighty-four years, who . . . served God with fastings and prayers night and day. And coming in that instant she gave thanks to the Lord, and spoke of Him to all those who looked for redemption in Jerusalem.

LUKE 2:36–38

"Your very words condemn you, old woman."

"No." Anna nearly shouted. "My words condemn you! The One who will redeem Jerusalem has been born. Pray you do not live long enough to see him return as a man to this very place!"

They advanced on her.

"You will strike me?" Anna asked boldly. "An old woman guarded only by a little girl?"

Her raised voice drew the attention of passersby. The men stopped, embarrassed.

"Come," Anna said to Marianne. "We will not give them the satisfaction of putting us in the hands of the temple police."

As slowly as they had arrived, the girl and the old woman began to walk away from the Court of Women.

"Do not fear for me," Anna assured Marianne. "God will hear my prayers no matter where I stand."

 She hugged the little girl. "As for you, long after I am gone, there will come a day when you will hear of a man named Yeshua. When you do, you must follow him. He is the hope that has taken away all my sadness."

Young as she was, Marianne heard truth and joy in the old woman's words.

The old woman leaned on her shoulder and Marianne helped her walk at a slow, steady pace away from the priests . . . toward the hope that each one of them now carried deep within.

No Ordinary Boy

This is no ordinary boy.

Around him are his parents and their friends and their families. Together, they have traveled many days south to Jerusalem from their small village in the hills of Galilee.

 They are surrounded by hundreds of other pilgrims arriving for the yearly Passover ceremonies. Like the boy, many of them are seeing the Temple for the first time. And like the boy, they have stopped to stare in wonder and awe.

Below them is the Kidron Valley, spanned by a high, wide bridge that reaches over an immense chasm to where the huge eastern wall of the Temple rises its sheer face 450 feet above the valley floor. (Some of the pilgrims whisper that from this pinnacle the blasphemous are hurled to their death on the rocks below.)

Beyond this massive wall, guarded by immense gates, is the Temple Mount. Its background—the upper city of the wealthy—is almost heavenly in appearance. Heat shimmers the boy's vision, and the white palaces and villa gardens seem to be a mirage oasis appearing from out of nowhere among the desert's brown hills and clear blue sky. Yet against this painting of magnificence, the Temple Mount dominates gloriously with its crown of burnished gold and glistening marble.

Few are those who can speak with more than hushed whispers upon seeing the Temple of Jerusalem for the first time.

In this regard, the boy from Nazareth is no different from others.

A CHILD'S VIEW OF JERUSALEM

A crowded city offers fascinating sights to any child, but to a child visiting from a small village, the city of Jerusalem during Passover would have been an awesome sight.

The upper city, the location of the wealthy, was filled with huge mansions and courtyards of beautiful gardens. The lower city was crowded with the poor.

The merchant streets, filled with the stalls of shoemakers, tailors, flax spinners, goldsmiths, wool combers, butchers, food inspectors, and diplomats, created a colorful bazaar. Among the warehouses and markets, the air would be filled with the smell of fish, incense, ripe and rotting fruit, and the stench of leather being cured and tanned and dyed.

Here the Passover pilgrims could find restaurants and wine shops, and partake from a selection of food—ranging from fried locusts to fresh and salted fish to fruit cakes—and drink, Judean or Galilean wine or a wide range of foreign beer.

Yes. He whispers. Quietly. Not even those who stand beside him hear the words he speaks to himself.

No, this is not an ordinary boy. While the vision of the Temple inspires wonder and awe in all who behold it, for this boy it inspires much more.

Something in him awakens. Something that has always been inside, murmuring comfort and calm peace. He stirs with excitement, in the way a weary sailor feels exhilaration when the distant shore of an almost forgotten home rises dimly on the horizon.

When the boy whispers—unlike any pilgrim before or after him—it is the whisper of a consciousness discovering renewed purpose. His words make sense only to himself. Indeed, in a few days time, this twelve-year-old boy will repeat them to his mother, and she will not understand.

But he understands. As does the One who sent him.

For he is no ordinary boy.

"This," he whispers with divine comprehension as the stunning beauty of the Temple overwhelms him, *"is my Father's house."*

It was not all pleasant, however. Danger also lurked in the city, both for children and for adults, because of thieves and prostitutes in the lower city, especially among the dark, underground tunnels. Later, when Jerusalem fell to the Roman siege, hundreds of people hid in these tunnels until hunger forced them into the open.

The city's architecture was impressive, even for sophisticated Romans, who could find distraction at the horse races in Herod's Hippodrome, or disappear into a theater, or lose themselves in hot steam baths as luxurious as any in Rome.

One of the most amazing sights in Jerusalem was the Temple. Covering over thirty-two acres, it was the most impressive building any visitor might see in a lifetime. It had nine gates that opened onto a large outer court—the Court of Gentiles—named so because anyone could enter. The individual building stones of the Temple were higher than a man could reach. The peak of the inner Temple was ten stories tall. The outer wall on one side plunged hundreds of feet to a valley below.

At any time, from any part of the city, the people could see continual smoke from sacrifices, rising above the temple altar like a curtain between earth and heaven—a constant reminder of God's presence.

His parents went to Jerusalem every year at the Feast of the Passover. And when He was twelve years old, they went up to Jerusalem according to the custom of the feast. . . . After three days they found Him in the temple, sitting in the midst of the teachers, both listening to them and asking them questions. And all who heard Him were astonished at His understanding and answers.

LUKE 2:41–42, 46–47

STICKS AND STONES

In a town like Nazareth, all the Jews gathered early on the Sabbath to worship at the synagogue. Inside the synagogue, a raised platform stood in front of the wall that faced Jerusalem. On the platform, a seven-branch candelabra illuminated a reading desk. A prayer leader, or *hazzan*, stood on the platform to direct the service. This prayer leader was not a priest but simply a respected man of the community.

After opening prayers, the *hazzan* brought from the back of the synagogue the Ark, a wooden chest that contained the Torah scroll (the books of Law). He would open the chest, lift out the Torah, slide it from its linen mantle, and unscroll the parchment on the reading desk. Then he would call various men to the platform to read different portions of the Law.

A voice at the front of the synagogue drones in the way it does every Sabbath to begin the service. The little boy Shimshai ignores it. A large beetle in front of him on the floor holds his attention. Perhaps if he slides his foot forward . . . Shimshai winces as his older brother's strong fingers dig into his tiny shoulders. He does not cry out in pain, however. At seven, Shimshai fully understands that noise must never disrupt the synagogue service. Both he and his brother understand how angry their father would be should either of them bring shame upon the family.

A few minutes later, his brother's hand falls off his shoulder, and Shimshai sighs a long breath of boredom. The reading of the Law is nearly complete. All of this he has heard before.

He drops his eyes to his feet, hoping the beetle has foolishly moved close enough to be discreetly tormented . . . perhaps even squashed. No such fortune. Keeping his head still to escape his brother's notice, Shimshai searches with his eyes. *Where has the beetle gone?*

Whispers ripple among the people, diverting Shimshai's attention as someone new approaches the lectern.

The sight of a familiar face disappoints him. It is only the son of Joseph, now invited to read the concluding portion, the *Haftarah*. Why then the whispers of excitement?

A woman, almost out of earshot, on the other side of a partition, answers indirectly. She speaks quietly to another woman.

"They say that in Cana last week he healed the son of an officer of Herod Antipas. Yet the son was at Capernaum!"

Shimshai forgets the beetle. He remembers a visit once to Capernaum. It is more than a day's travel away, on the shore of the Sea of Galilee, while Cana is a small village just down the road. *How could a healing take place across that distance?*

"And don't forget the wedding at Cana," the woman continues. "He hasn't been to Nazareth since."

"Don't believe that nonsense about the water and the wine," her friend replies, emboldened to speak aloud by the noise of other conversations that ripple across the synagogue. "It is a story of drunk revelers who were easily fooled. Now set a good example for the nearby children and listen. The service is nearly finished."

 When the carpenter's son speaks, Shimshai senses the attentiveness of the adults around him. Something about this man's presence fills the synagogue. Shimshai hears the richness in his voice as he recites from the scroll.

"The Spirit of the Lord is upon Me, because He has anointed Me to preach the gospel to the poor. He has sent me to proclaim liberty to the captives and recovery of sight to the blind, to set at liberty those who are oppressed, to proclaim the acceptable year of the Lord."

The carpenter's son finishes reading the words of Isaiah and rolls up the scroll. All eyes are upon him—including Shimshai's. He has seen the son of the carpenter many times before in the village, but now, somehow, the man seems different.

"Today," the man says, "this Scripture is fulfilled in your hearing." Shimshai is amazed—not at his words, but at the people around him

In Jesus' time, the classical Hebrew of the Torah was ancient and no longer spoken by the people, so the reader would pause while a translator recited the text in Aramaic. When the reading was complete, the speaker then gave a commentary or sermon on the passage. Depending on the Sabbath, the people might listen to three or more lengthy lessons.

After reading from the books of Law, another man from the community concluded the service by reading from one of the prophetic books of the Bible, as Jesus did when he was invited to read from Isaiah. Finally, the *hazzan* gave a benediction, and with the exchange of Sabbath good wishes the service ended.

who respond with outbursts of whispered conversations, not even bothering a pretense of politeness. Even the elders have forgotten the importance of synagogue silence.

"What words of grace!" someone says.

"And to think this is only Joseph's son!" replies another.

"He speaks with such authority!"

"Amazing! Where did he learn this?"

"Remember the miracles!"

"If he has done that in other towns, surely he will favor us with even more!"

 Shimshai hears the nearby woman again, and giggles, for this woman allows that the carpenter's son, no longer a nobody in the village, is now a suitable husband for her daughter.

"Heal someone!" a man shouts in excitement. "Turn water into wine!"

Others take up the call. Shimshai finds himself gleefully shouting aloud with his brother; they see ahead that their father has joined in the commotion, too.

Finally, the carpenter's son speaks again. This time, there is no calm authority in his voice, but anger. Shimshai shrinks back, clutching his brother's hand in fear, as the carpenter's son chastises the entire Nazareth synagogue for seeking a miracle worker instead of understanding his true mission.

There is silence again. A shocked silence. It does not last long. Shimshai holds his brother's hand tighter as the grumbling around them turns to complaints, the complaints to criticism, and the criticism to fury.

He came to Nazareth, where He had been brought up. And as His custom was, He went into the synagogue on the Sabbath day, and stood up to read. And He was handed the book of the prophet Isaiah. . . . And He began to say to them, "Today this Scripture is fulfilled in your hearing." . . . So all those in the synagogue, when they heard these things, were filled with wrath, and rose up and thrust Him out of the city; and they led Him to the brow of the hill on which their city was built, that they might throw Him down over the cliff.

LUKE 4:16–17, 21, 28–30

Shimshai is nearly knocked over as the adults drive the carpenter's son from the synagogue down the road to the brow of the hill overlooking Nazareth. On the road, Shimshai stays near his parents—amazed and delighted that they have joined in the angry shouts and fist-shaking as the mob thrusts the carpenter's son closer and closer to a cliff on the western side of the town.

Caught up in this incredible hysteria, Shimshai picks up a stone to hurl at the man. This is far more exciting than tormenting a beetle.

Ahead is a cliff, one that will surely mean death for the man. Shimshai has never seen a man die; he is fascinated and curious by the tumult in front of him. From earliest childhood he has been warned about the penalty for blasphemy. What will it look like when the man's body tumbles onto the rocks below?

Then something happens that Shimshai will remember for the rest of his life.

 The people stop. Their shouts cease. They step aside to make a path down the middle of the crowd . . . and the man walks through as if an unspoken command grips every person in the crowd. Many around him release their sticks and stones.

As the man passes by, his eyes drop to the rock in Shimshai's small fist. Those eyes lift again and pierce Shimshai with pity and sadness. Shimshai, shaken with sudden understanding, opens his small fist. The rock in his fingers falls at his feet.

He watches the man walk away from the crowd without looking back, unharmed.

Shimshai will never speak of this to anyone, but until his death, every Sabbath will bring to his heart a knot of sorrow and regret. How he will wish he had never picked up that rock.

Shimshai's sorrow and regret will not be wasted, however. As a grown man in front of his own children, he will carefully guard his every action—for he will always remember, too well, how easily the young learn by example.

DAUGHTER

Rachel recognized the clothing, the stooped shoulders, even the shape of the hooded head. She had seen this man from a distance many times in the countryside, well outside the town walls. But she was not permitted to approach him, much as she ached to be near him.

Her father.

As he approached, the other women at the well sprang to their feet, ending their gossip with cries of horror.

"Stay back!" a woman cried at the figure. "Leave us alone!"

Still, the figure approached. Women gathered their skirts in their hands and ran, kicking dust in the air. Many left their buckets behind.

But Rachel remained. She had only one bucket, now full of water. It was all she could carry with her thin arms and thin shoulders. Though her mother and smaller sisters were waiting for the water, amazed disbelief kept her rooted at the side of the well.

Her father?

Night after night, she cried herself to sleep thinking of him. She had been seven when the discolored blotches first appeared on his arms and face. Within days, a sharp-eyed villager had noticed, and that same morning a priest had appeared at their doorstep. Swift judgment had been rendered.

Leprosy. Living death!

Two years ago Rachel had clung to her father's leg as he left their

---

JESUS' MIRACLES

The Gospel writers speak of many miracles performed by Jesus during his time on earth. They were so numerous that sheer practicality forced the writers to be selective about which miracles they described, for "if they were written one by one, . . . even the world itself could not contain the books that would be written" (John 21:25).

The range of miracles shows that Jesus helped people as diverse as family and friends (Peter's mother-in-law; Lazarus), to foreigners (a Canaanite woman's daughter; a Greek man possessed by demons). Jesus helped the hated Romans (the centurion's servant) and respected Jews (synagogue ruler Jairus and his daughter). Jesus healed men and women, young and old, officials in high positions and officials' servants.

The selection of miracles recorded in the Gospels gives us a clear sense of Jesus' true mission of love—he helped people without regard to nationality, race, or religion, simply because they needed his help.

household for the last time. He had turned upon her with an anger she had never heard in his voice before, shouting that she could never come near him again.

No one in the village could. And that is why she cried herself to sleep at night. It hurt to think of her father despised and alone.

 She saw him in the distance from time to time, often enough to know what his life was like. Wearing the clothes of a mourner, he declared his own death while he still lived. Crying out, "unclean, unclean," as demanded by the Law, served both as a warning and as a plea for the listeners' prayers.

Her father was banished. So close . . . yet so far away.

During the past two years, Rachel's mother had gone outside the village to leave him food at a pre-arranged spot whenever they had extra. She always went alone and always returned with tears pouring from her red-rimmed eyes.

And now her father approached.

Rachel wavered as she moved toward him. "Father?"

He stopped from habit. Ceremonial law declared that no one could stand closer than four cubits to a leper.

"Rachel? My daughter?" His voice nearly broke. "Surely that cannot be you. You have grown. You look so much like your mother."

"Father?"

"The man did not drive me away," came the voice from within the hood. "I had no right even to speak to him, yet he did not drive me away."

And behold, a leper came and worshiped
Him, saying, "Lord, if You are willing,
You can make me clean."

Then Jesus put out His hand and touched
him, saying, "I am willing; be cleansed."
Immediately his leprosy was cleansed.

MATTHEW 8:2–3

"Who, father?" Rachel's legs seemed hardly capable of holding her upright, let alone taking her with trembling steps toward the ragged figure.

"He touched me," her father said. "Any man who touches me becomes unclean . . . yet . . . he touched me!"

"Who father?" Rachel had stepped within the four cubits. She had once seen another leper. She had seen the fingerless hands, the stumped feet. Yet she was not revolted at the thought of holding her own dear father, no matter what leprosy had done to him. If only he would let her.

"A man from Nazareth. The one named Jesus. He sent me to the priest. That is where I go now. I must go to the priest, before I return to our home. It would be too cruel to give false hope."

"Father?" Rachel moved closer. The stench of his rags made her blink.

Yes, young as she was, she knew enough of lepers to know how the ulcers of the skin discharged a pus that soaked their clothing. How for some, the eyebrows rotted away; how the voice became hoarse and wheezing.

Her father smelled of discharge, yet his voice was the voice she remembered. How could this be?

"Father?"

He stretched his hands from the sleeves of his dirty, ragged clothing. He held them up to the shadows of his hooded face and turned them in the sunlight.

"Look," he said. "They are whole."

She took another step toward him.

"No," he said. "Not yet. Not until we know I am healed."

Rachel waited. She hugged herself with her tiny thin arms.

"Dare I show you what I cannot see for myself?" he asked. "Dare I ask you to examine my own face? You . . . a child?"

"Yes, father," Rachel answered. "Please."

He lifted a hand toward his head. Healthy, strong fingers clenched the edge of the hood.

What would she see? The thick nodules of a leper's face, oozing with pus? A nose rotted and disfigured? Would she see what he had never wanted her to see—the face of a monster?

He lifted the hood back.

Rachel stared, frozen for a moment by what she saw.

The she flung herself into his arms. He held her tight, knowing there would be time to visit the priest later.

 In his arms, her small body shook with unrestrained sobs of joy. She had seen her father smile. The smile she remembered every night as she wept for him. The smile that belonged to her now, once again.

A GIFT RETURNED

The sun burns down on brown hills. The wide valley is filled with a haze of heat. There is nothing to suggest to the women that this day in their tiny village in the hills of Judea will be any different from every other day with its rhythm of toil from dawn's first light to the last rays of sunset.

They brought little children to Him, that He might touch them . . .

MARK 10:13

 Then, at the village well, word of the Rabbi's approach first reaches the women. They are helping each other draw water with heavy buckets—a daily necessity that is also an excuse to get into the sunshine, away from oppressive work in often oppressive patriarchal homes.

The Rabbi Yeshua! A man who heals! A man who defies the synagogues and actually teaches women!

It is curiosity that draws most of the women to leave the well and approach the crowd around him. But the women do not walk alone. They carry their babies, or hold the hands of the little ones who can walk, or call for the older children to follow.

Because they are merely women, they must remain at the back of the crowd. They stand on their toes to get a glimpse of Jesus over the heads of the men in front. They strain to hear snatches of his conversation.

Mutters passed along by the crowd reach them as they tend their children.

Shammai, the village's most self-righteous, priggish Pharisee—a leering white-haired goat of a man who prays publicly yet clutches at women in the crowded market—has just challenged the Rabbi Yeshua on how a man may put away his wife.

The women—who at one time or another have all suffered Shammai's private advances but are unable to tell their husbands for fear of being accused of encouraging another man—listen intently for Jesus' answer. They are resigned to whatever answer he might give. After all, in Jewish law, a woman was regarded merely as a *thing*.

She had no legal rights. According to the school of Hillel scholars, if a wife spoiled a dish of food, if she spun wool in the streets, even if she spoke to an unfamiliar man, a husband could divorce her. Left poor and alone, discarded as "used goods," she would have no respectful way to earn a living. It was such a pitiful situation that many women hesitated to marry at all.

To the amazement of the women at the back of the crowd, they clearly hear anger in Jesus' reply—anger at the men as he tells them that Moses wrote the law because of the hardness of their hearts. Anger as he tells them with a mantle of divine authority that what God has joined together no man should separate.

What a radical, powerful declaration for women and the unity of the family! What a gift of freedom! The women can hardly believe what they hear!

Some of the women find courage in Jesus' words.

Enough courage to push through the crowd. Enough courage to endure the jostling and stares and rude comments of Shammai and the other Pharisees.

They push forward, cradling their babies and little children in their arms, protecting little boys and girls from the sharp elbows and hardshoulders of the men who would deny them a chance to meet this great teacher.

When they reach Jesus, they lift their children into his arms, crowding in tight all around him.

As women, they have nothing more important than their children, no gift more precious to offer to this Man of love.

He takes the children into his arms, holds them close, and blesses them.

THE PARALYZED MAN

Phylo sat on the sea wall at every opportunity, simply because watching the boats leave and return from the pier was the most interesting activity he found in Capernaum.

All of the fishermen knew him and kept a watchful eye out for him, this one they called with some degree of affection "the little Greek scavenger." Phylo was small and fast and, when possible, followed the men when they shouldered their baskets, darting beneath their feet to steal any fish that fell to the ground. The fishermen would shout angry threats in the boy's direction, but they found it difficult to sustain anger against his wide, ready smile and laughter as he ran away from them.

This morning the fishing masts were all on the horizon, and Phylo kicked the back of his heels against the sea wall in boredom.

Suddenly he spotted four Jews walking awkwardly together as they carried a load between them. From a distance, Phylo knew they were Jews because of the *sudar* each wore, a kerchief twisted into a turban to cover the head.

Phylo pushed off the sea wall and hopped to his feet. Something odd was going on here—something that was sure to break his spell of boredom.

Each of the four men carried the corner of a mat. A fifth man lay in the center of the mat, his head looking too large above his frail body. All of them had sparse beards, the efforts of young men trying to appear older.

Phylo moved closer to them.

"Taking him to the market to sell as a slave?" Phylo asked with a laugh. He knew he was safe. None of the four would be able to drop a corner of the mat to chase him; if one did, Phylo was certain he could outrun any pursuer.

To Phylo's disappointment, the men chose to ignore him. He didn't get any reaction from them, not even a grunt of acknowledgment. They were intent on their destination, whatever it was.

Phylo followed, skipping circles around them. The four men continued eastward, along the sea wall toward the houses in the Jewish part of town.

"Perhaps then," Phylo addressed the frail man on the mat, "these four are your slaves. I would suggest, however, that a chariot might be more comfortable!"

"Hush, little fly," one of the men on the corners snapped. "We have matters far more important than you to attend to."

Phylo laughed, delighted to have provoked them at last.

He spent the next five minutes lunging close, and just as swiftly retreating, again and again, even going so far as to tug on their robes before dancing out of reach.

What fun! What helpless victims!

The four men rounded a corner with their burden. Phylo still buzzed around them. Ahead was a large crowd, spilling into the narrow street before a house just down from the synagogue.

Phylo stopped abruptly, trying to make sense of it all. The Jewish men moved forward, pausing at the edge of the crowd to set the mat gently on the ground.

"What now?" the man on the mat said. "We'll never get inside to see him."

Phylo was close enough to hear the sorrow and defeat in the frail man's voice.

"Who?" Phylo asked, edging closer, trying to peer between the crowded bodies ahead of him. What kind of man would draw such a crowd? And for what reason? In his curiosity, tiny Phylo forgot the nearness of the four Jews he had been teasing.

One of them grabbed him by his shoulders, and dangled him in the air.

"None of your business, street rat." They were face to face. Phylo could see no real anger in the man's face. He gave him a wide, charming grin, knowing that only the worst of bullies would harm a small boy like himself.

The Jew shook his head in disgust and dropped Phylo. "Bah. Run back to your mother."

Phylo didn't run, however.

"Who is inside?" he asked again. "And why have you brought your friend to see him?"

Phylo's earnest seriousness, in such contrast to his banter and teasing, must have made an impression on the man who had just dropped him.

"Jesus of Nazareth," the man answered. "A man who can heal our friend."

"Heal your friend?" Phylo almost laughed, but he was watching the desperate hope on the face of the paralyzed man. Impudent and saucy as he was, even Phylo sensed this was not a moment for mockery.

"That is why the crowd is so large," the man said.

"Everybody wants to see him."

Phylo looked at the crowd. Looked at the house. *Heal a paralyzed man? Impossible. But it was worth trying to see. No matter what!*

"How will the five of us ever push our way through that crowd?" one of the men asked the others. "This is impossible!"

"Well," Phylo said, with the mind of the audacious escape artist that he was, "what about the outer staircase?"

"The staircase?"

"It leads to the roof," Phylo said. "From there you could remove some of the tiles, and lower your friend down inside, couldn't you?"

The four men looked at each other, with full seconds passing as first they exchanged frowns . . . then . . . grins.

The one who had grabbed Phylo laughed aloud. "The street rat has value after all!"

He stopped abruptly. "That is," he said, looking down at the frail man on the mat, "if you agree. After all, it will cause a commotion. And nothing may result from all of this. If the miracles are nothing but rumor . . ."

 The frail man with the large head and sparse beard smiled sadly. "All my life, when I've heard stories about others daring to take a risk, I've wondered how it might feel . . . wondered if *I* would ever have such courage."

He slowly nodded his head. "Yes," he said, "take me to the roof. Let me down in front of this man Jesus. If all fails, even if the people laugh, at least I will always know that at least once I, too, dared to risk."

The four Jewish men each grabbed a corner of the mat and lifted their friend toward the stairs. Phylo watched from a distance as they struggled up the stairs and began to break up the tiles on the roof.

He paced at the edges of the crowd, anxious to know what was happening.

Waiting . . . waiting . . . waiting.

 Finally, he could stand it no longer. He darted up the stairs and reached the roof just as the four began to lower their friend through the hole where they had broken pieces of clay from the supporting framework.

Phylo grinned. His idea had worked!

But his grin quickly faded . . . *How could the sickly, frail man ever walk again? Surely he was in for a big disappointment . . .*

Phylo crept closer to the four men. He dropped to his knees and peered between their legs.

Words reached him.

Sins . . . forgiven.

Blasphemy . . . only God . . .

What is easier. . . sins forgiven . . . or get up and walk?

I have authority on earth . . .

Then came the words that filled Phylo with awe every time he remembered them.

Stand up, take your mat, and go home, because you are healed.

Still on his knees, Phylo pushed closer, almost falling over the edge of the broken roof in his enthusiasm to see what would happen next.

The frail man with the large head stood up! He actually stood on his short, thin legs . . . like a newborn calf . . . wobbly yet triumphant.

He stood! He wept! He clutched people around him with joy!

Then, remembering the words of Jesus, the man took up his mat. Slowly, he pushed his way through the crowd, a crowd babbling with excitement, parting for him now as if for an apparition.

Later, Phylo told himself, later he would find out everything he could about this man who worked miracles.

But for now, he wanted to be the first to greet the man with the mat.

Phylo raced back down the stairs ahead of the four men, whooping with excitement. What a man, this Jesus!

Behold, men brought on a bed a man who was paralyzed, whom they sought to bring in and lay before Him. And when they could not find how they might bring him in, because of the crowd, they went up on the housetop and let him down with his bed through the tiling into the midst before Jesus. He said to the man who was paralyzed, "I say to you, arise, take up your bed, and go to your house." Immediately he rose up before them, took up what he had been lying on, and departed to his own house, glorifying God.

LUKE 5: 18-19, 24-25

A SABBATH OF HOPE

It was no light question when the Pharisees asked Jesus if it was lawful to heal on the Sabbath. Some forms of desecration of the Sabbath were a crime for which a man or woman might be stoned to death.

Moreover, dozens of laws minutely detailed what consisted of work on a Sabbath. It was forbidden to eat an egg laid on the Sabbath by a hen kept expressly for laying, for the hen had worked; had the hen been one kept only for fattening the egg could be consumed because it was considered a part of the hen that had fallen off.

If a man's house caught fire on the Sabbath, it was considered work to attempt to put it out—but if a neighbor who was a Gentile attempted to extinguish the flames without being asked it was permitted. Furthermore, of the possessions inside a burning house, a Jew could only remove what was essential for food and drink that day, for carrying anything else was considered work.

Tola and Tamar hold hands, squeezing tightly.

At any other time, in any other situation, Tola, who is eleven and proud to be his father's only son, would never hold his little sister's hand in public. Now, however, in this moment of suspense, he scarcely notices that each has reached for the other.

They stand at the rear of the synagogue, separate from the adults. While their vision of the lectern is partially obscured by the heads and shoulders of the men seated in front, in the hushed silence they hear clearly every word that is spoken.

Is it lawful to heal on the Sabbath?

The boy and girl know that two men stand at the front, drawing the attention of a packed synagogue: a man named Jesus . . . and their father.

They had watched their father make his way forward, risking public humiliation and the wrath of the town's elders, simply because he wanted to be able to provide for his family. A man with a useless hand can find little work.

Is it lawful to heal on the Sabbath?

Neither Tola nor Tamar care that this is a showdown between a rebel miracle–worker and the judges and arbitrators of orthodox morality. Neither do they know that their father is being used as a pawn in the showdown.

All they care about, during the moment of silence that follows the question, is how much they love their father, how much it hurts day by day to see his dejection and discouragement when he returns to their simple home each night with meager rations of coarse barley bread and salted fish.

Is it lawful to heal on the Sabbath?

Finally Jesus breaks the silence—by answering with questions of his own. In a warm, vibrant voice he directs compassion toward their father, "Would not any man lift a sheep out of a pit on the Sabbath?" . . . and anger at the Pharisees, "And how much more is a man worth than a sheep?"

Tola and Tamar are far too young to realize that the questions Jesus poses in front of this rapt audience strike deep at generations of legalism, breaking the clay of man-made rabbinic law to expose the shining metal of biblical law underneath. *Is it not evil to ignore the chance to do good?*

Tola and Tamar simply clutch each other tighter in hope and fear.

Can this Jesus help their father? *Will* he help their father?

Suddenly they hear the words they will never forget.

"Stretch forth your hand."

Tola and Tamar do not see the emotions cross their father's face as he struggles with a decision. If he obeys and is not healed, he will be humiliated even more, doomed to be mocked in their small village for the rest of his life. But if he lets fear of the elders stop him from listening to the compassion in Jesus' words . . . and trusting that Jesus is truly able to heal him . . .

As for healing, a bandage could be applied to a wound on the condition it was to prevent the wound from getting worse; efforts to heal the wound by applying salve or a plaster or any other medical attention must wait until the Sabbath ended.

Thus, in healing the man with the withered hand, Jesus doubly enraged the Pharisees. By posing his question about helping a sheep on the Sabbath, by asking if it was lawful to do good or evil, to save a life or to kill, Jesus had shown the entire audience the depth of their mean-spirited pettiness. And, to frustrate them more, in healing the man, Jesus had not broken the law in any way that would allow the Pharisees to rebuke him, for Jesus had not touched the man. He had not applied a plaster, a salve, an ointment or bandage, all of which would break any of the myriad of Sabbath decrees. He had only asked the man to stretch forth his hand. By their own precious laws, the Pharisees could find no recourse to condemn Jesus. All they could do from that point on was to plot how they might kill him.

Tola and Tamar do not see their father stretch forth his hand in an act of faith. Nor do they see—unexplainable as it might be—when the withered flesh becomes strong again . . . when fingers curled with atrophy suddenly flex with stunned joy.

But they do hear gasps of awe, exultations of joy.

For all the others in the synagogue, when the astounded cries echo to silence, the drama is over. The Pharisees will leave the synagogue to plot other ways of ending Christ's ministry, and Jesus himself will move on to other towns and villages, teaching and healing.

Yet of all the people involved in that Sabbath drama, Jesus, in his infinite love and wisdom, is the one who understands fully what he will leave behind, what his act of love means to the father and the children.

 For when all have cleared the synagogue, there remains only the man and his young son holding tightly to the hand of his daughter. In the silence the man holds out his own hands, marveling at their new strength. Where once his fingers were powerless, a crippled mass of claws, he is finally able to do what his heart has longed to do since their births.

He traces the smiles of his children with the fingers of his hand.

He went into their synagogue. And behold, there was a man who had a withered hand. And they asked Him, saying, "Is it lawful to heal on the Sabbath?"—that they might accuse Him. . . . Then He said to the man, "Stretch out your hand." And he stretched it out, and it was restored as whole as the other.

MATTHEW 12:9–10, 13–14

A DESPERATE FATHER

His slim back to the doorway, Tobiah stood at the window overlooking the Sea of Galilee. He gazed over the rooftops scattered below across the hillside and at the calm waters beyond. Far away, the southern hills were a smudge against the horizon.

 A day of sunshine, the blue sky was reflected in the water. He wondered if it would be worth the effort of going down to the market of Capernaum. Rarely did he find anything worth purchasing; yet sickness had kept him away from the market for several days, and he was feeling bored.

Yes, Tobiah decided. He would go to the market, if only to ensure that the household servants were buying the freshest of foods.

Tobiah lifted a silver bell. With a practiced flick of the wrist, he rang it loudly.

He began a slow count. *"One . . . two . . ."*

Finally, a servant pushed through the doorway curtain.

"Master!" the servant gasped. He was a large man, with a wide scar across his nose. From a sword in battle or a similar dreary tale, Tobiah recalled, but what else did one expect from an older slave captured from some barbaric country too far away to bother remembering?

". . . ten . . . ," Tobiah said. "I was past a count of ten! Were you asleep?"

"No," the servant said. "I just did not expect to hear the bell.

You were . . . you were . . . you . . ."

The servant swung his head around, turning to look at the crumpled linens where Tobiah had been tossing in fevered unconsciousness. "What I mean was that . . . ," the servant took a deep breath, "I did not expect you to have risen from your fever . . . and . . . and here you are, walking!"

"Here I am," Tobiah snapped, "standing only in my undergarments. Where are my clothes?"

"Clothes?" If the burly servant felt any insult at the arrogant tone of a twelve–year–old Jew chastising him, he hid it carefully. The master of the household was an official who reported directly to Herod Antipas. Both Herod and the master were unpredictable, men with power who acted upon whims. And Tobiah had repeatedly shown a strong inclination to walk doggedly in their footsteps. "Clothes?"

"I wish to visit the market," Tobiah said. "Fetch my clothes, immediately. And bring a jug of water. I am thirsty."

Tobiah frowned, and put up a hand to stop the servant from leaving. "Where is my father?"

"He has gone to Cana," the servant replied.

"Cana? That's a full day's travel. What business was important enough to take him away from Capernaum when I was so sick?"

"He . . . we . . . all feared for your life. For two days, you were senseless with fever. Your father was so desperate that when he heard of the miracle worker—"

"Miracle worker? What superstitious nonsense is this? No respected Jew would stoop to seeking a miracle worker." Slight as he was, Tobiah was able to project a bullying authority with ease.

"Your father was very worried. I believe he felt there was nowhere else to turn." Indeed, it was the only time the servant could remember that the master had shown any humility or fear. So much so that all the servants in the household felt pity for the distraught man.

"A miracle worker?" Tobiah repeated.

"From Nazareth. One named Yeshuah. He has returned to Galilee from the region of Judea, and already has a great following. Your father hoped to bring him here to heal you."

Tobiah laughed. "Heal me? What nonsense. Look at me. I am completely well. I have no need of healing."

The servant nodded. Yes, it was obvious that the irritating boy was completely well and able to resume terrorizing the household.

"Hurry then," Tobiah said. "My clothes. A cloak. And a jug of water. I wish to waste no time. The best wares at the market will already be gone."

Tobiah glanced out the window to judge the height of the sun.

"Hurry!" he snapped again at the servant. "If my guess is correct, we are already into the seventh hour."

The servant made note of that. Undoubtedly, he would be sent down the road to find the master and give him the news that his desperate search for the miracle worker named Yeshua was no longer necessary. Tobiah's health had returned of its own accord in the seventh hour.

Yes, the servant thought with some dismay, much as the master will take joy in the good news, he will still be irritated that the entire two-day journey to Cana and back home had been wasted.

Unless . . .

There was a certain nobleman whose son was sick at Capernaum. When he heard that Jesus had come out of Judea into Galilee, he went to Him and implored Him to come down and heal his son, for he was at the point of death. . . . Jesus said to him, "Go your way; your son lives." So the man believed the word that Jesus spoke to him, and he went his way. And as he was now going down, his servants met him and told him, saying, "Your son lives!" Then he inquired of them the hour when he got better. And they said to him, "Yesterday at the seventh hour the fever left him." So the father knew that it was at the same hour in which Jesus said to him, "Your son lives."

JOHN 4:47-53

No. The servant shook off a stray thought. *It was not possible for any miracle worker to heal the boy from a distance—not unless the man was God Himself.*

Tobiah's voice startled the servant out of his ponderings.

"Water! Immediately! I die of thirst and you do nothing!"

"Yes, yes," the servant said, hurrying out of the room.

Like father, like son. It was one thing for the fever to break in the seventh hour . . . it would be another if these two ever learned anything about kindness and love.

As the servant filled a jug with water for the spoiled boy, he permitted himself a wry smile of disbelief. *Actually, there wasn't much chance of either miracle . . . was there?*

One time Zeno saw the man cut himself with shards of rock.

Zeno thought of the wild man now. Surely the sound of the splashing of oars would catch his attention and draw him out from the tombs, where he slept among the cloth-tattered bones of the long-dead.

Sound carried so well across the cove that Zeno could hear the rasping of the boat's bottom as it was dragged onto the narrow shoreline. Sure enough, he did not have to wait long for the wild man to appear.

Like a jagged shadow, the wild man staggered from side to side, running and waving his arms to scare off the men in the boat.

Zeno could not imagine what would happen when the poor man met up with those men. Someone would surely get hurt.

Then something totally unexpected happened.

Suddenly, the wild man fell to his knees as the figure in the bow of the boat stepped down onto the shore.

"What do you want with me?" the wild man screamed. "What do you want with me, Jesus, Son of the Most High God?"

The wild man's words confused Zeno. He knew of no "Jesus" among the gods of the Greek temples of Decapolis. He leaned forward, determined not to miss a word and nearly jumped when a hand rested on his shoulder.

"What is it?" a low voice whispered. It was one of the other swineherds, drawn to the cliff by the shouting below.

Zeno didn't answer but merely pointed down to the cove. Together, they watched and listened.

"Come out of this man, you evil spirit," the man from the boat

THE YOUNGEST SWINEHERD

The sound of splashing water roused Zeno from sleep. He was curled against a boulder at the top edge of the cliff, buried within a heavy coat. He blinked, not looking down at the lake waters but instinctively surveying the hillside behind him.

All was in order. The pigs—hundreds upon hundreds of low curved shadows barely visible on the dark hill against the night sky—seemed calm. At the edges of the herd he saw the taller outlines of the other swineherds, leaning on their walking sticks as they waited out the monotony of the night watch.

Had anyone seen him dozing? He wondered to himself. He hoped not. As the youngest of the swineherds, he did not want to suffer their ridicule. To them he was only a boy; it seemed he was constantly trying to prove otherwise.

More splashing drew his attention back to the water below. The rhythmic dipping of oars carried clearly across the still of the night.

Zeno squinted harder. Then he saw it . . . almost a ghostly sight . . . the moonlight pale against a boat as it approached the narrow ledge of shore at the bottom of the cliffs. A man stood at the prow, like a statue, while other men huddled in the depths of the boat.

Zeno rubbed his eyes. Didn't these people know they were approaching a cliff side riddled with tombs? And in the dark of night?

Zeno forgot about the night chill as he watched intently. Among the tombs lived a wild man who shrieked and screamed at all hours of the night. He roamed free as the townspeople could no longer bind him.

DECAPOLIS

Located south and southeast of the Sea of Galilee, the region of Decapolis—"Ten Cities"—was made up of Greek cities that were subject to the Governor of Syria. Although this area was within the boundaries of ancient Israel, its population was heavily heathen. There were many temples built for the worship of Greek gods.

During this period of his ministry, Jesus wisely avoided traveling in Galilee, where many people wanted to force him to become their king, and where the actual king (more specifically, the tetrarch), Herod Antipas, was growing more hostile to Jesus' increasing influence.

commanded. He spoke with a heavy Galilean accent.

"I beg you!" the wild man shouted in return. "Do not torture me!"

The voices dropped as both men engaged in conversation. Zeno strained, but could not make out the words.

Then again, the frenzied shouting. "Do not torture us. Do not send us into the abyss!"

Zeno half turned with a question for the older herdsman beside him, but he didn't get the opportunity to ask.

"Send us among the pigs!" the wild man shouted. His screeching voice floating up from the dark shore was so eerie that shivers tightened the back of Zeno's neck. Much as he insisted to the other herders that he was a man, at this moment he truly felt like a small, frightened boy.

Without warning, the pigs behind him started to squeal, a sound like a high-pitched human scream.

Zeno turned. *This could not be! Surely it was only coincidence. Surely the man from the boat had nothing to do with this!*

Yet the squealing continued as the pigs began to shift and turn and mass together. Other herdsmen ran from all corners of the hill, trying to separate the pigs by beating them with their sticks. But their efforts were useless against the growing panic of the herd.

Then, to Zeno's horror, the dark, low mass of shadows suddenly bolted toward *him*.

"Run!" the herdsman beside him shouted. "Run!"

Zeno needed no further encouragement. The wild, squealing herd was thundering toward the cliff's edge—and he was squarely in their way!

Zeno barely had time to jump into a small protective ravine. He could

When He had come out of the boat, immediately there met Him out of the tombs a man with an unclean spirit, who had his dwelling among the tombs; and no one could bind him, not even with chains. . . .

[Jesus] said to him, "Come out of the man, unclean spirit!" . . . Now a large herd of swine was feeding there near the mountains. So all the demons begged [Jesus], saying, "Send us to the swine, that we may enter them. And at once Jesus gave them permission. Then the unclean spirit went out and entered the swine (there were about two thousand); and the herd ran violently down the steep place into the sea, and drowned in the sea.

So those who fed the swine fled, and they told it in the city and in the country.

MARK 5:2–14

hear the rough hides of the pigs brushing against each other as they swept over the side of the cliff. Like dominoes, the pressure of the pigs at the rear of the herd forced the ones at the front to tumble down the cliff, shrieking as they fell. It seemed that hours passed before the last pig plunged off the edge.

 The other herdsmen gathered with Zeno as they watched the thrashing animals in the lake below, churning the water into a phosphorescence of white bubbles that shone starkly against the waves in the moonlight.

No one said a word. Not one brash oath broke the silence. The herdsmen were too stunned to speak. When the last squealing pig disappeared beneath the black surface of the lake, the silence that fell upon them was as eerie as the moonlight on the bare hillsides.

Not even the wild man made any noise. Gone were his frenzied shoutings and lunatic dances. Instead, down on the narrow beach, he was on his knees near this Jesus, shoulders bowed as if in prayer.

A delayed reaction of terror took hold of Zeno. He did not care if the men around him thought of him as a boy, he turned and ran. Sheer terror drove him to run faster and faster away from the hillside, away from the wild man and the stampeding pigs. Away from the man in the boat. Whoever he was, he was a man to be feared. It did little to comfort Zeno that the men beside him were also running with terror.

Jesus. Son of the Most High God.

As Zeno ran and stumbled and ran across the uneven hillside those words echoed through his head again and again and again.

Jesus. Son of the Most High God.

Even evil spirits obeyed him. What did all of this mean?

There was one thing he knew for sure. Everyone must be warned!

FLUTES FOR THE DEAD

One of the rulers of the synagogue came, Jairus by name. And when he saw [Jesus], he fell at His feet and begged Him earnestly, saying, "My little daughter lies at the point of death. Come and lay Your hands on her, that she may be healed, and she will live." So Jesus went with him . . . .

Then [Jesus] took the child by the hand and said to her, "Talitha, cumi," which is translated, "Little girl, I say to you, arise." Immediately the girl arose and walked, for she was twelve years of age. And they were overcome with great amazement.

MARK 5:22-24, 41-42

She was twelve. Wrapped in bed linens, she lay pale and still. Her long, dark hair, damp from fever, was plastered to her face and skull.

During her last gasps for air, she did not hear her father leave the house, already sorry he had waited to the point of desperation to beg from the One who might save her.

She did not hear the cry of anguish as her mother held her limp hand and felt her life finally slip away.

She did not hear the wails of those who sorrowed for a girl so young, so beautiful—never to smile or sing, never to marry or hold a baby of her own.

She did not hear the melancholy mourning flutes, the flutes of the dead.

She did not hear the servants tell her father it was too late.

She did not hear the words of comfort to her father: "Do not be afraid; just believe."

She did not hear the scornful laughter as the gathered mourners mocked One who calmly said she was asleep.

She did not hear the tender words between her father and mother as they accompanied a Man of love and walked quietly with him into the room to view her lifeless body.

Yet when this Man took her hand and spoke, from somewhere beyond human understanding, she heard a voice of infinite love.

"Little girl, I say to you, get up."

This was the voice of the One who gives hope beyond death to all. She heard his voice. And she rose.

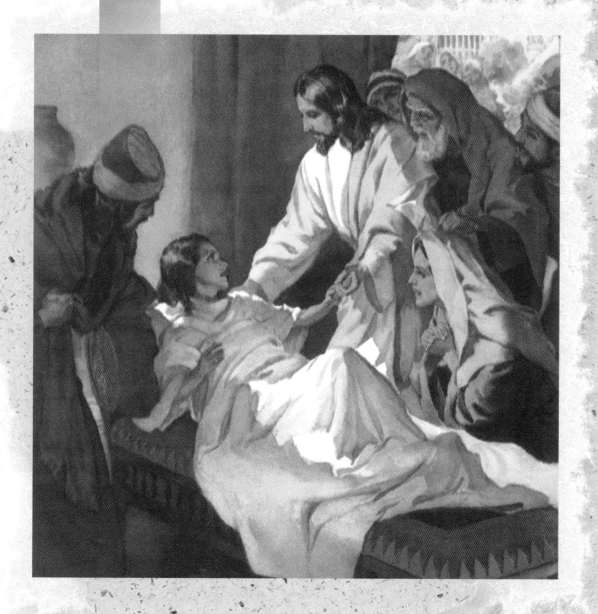

A FISHERMAN'S SON

Eli closed his eyes and leaned back against the ribs of the boat. The warmth of the sun on his face, the gentle rocking of the anchored boat, and the knowledge that he had little responsibility for the next few hours—all of it soothed him. He was going to sleep. Then eat his lunch. Then sleep some more.

Yes, he told himself as settled back to enjoy his nap, what could be better? Other boys his age toiled in the fields, cracking their fingernails on rocks and blistering their palms on wooden handles, but the son of a fisherman enjoyed the freedom of the wind and the water.

He settled into drowsy contentment . . . until an irritating buzz broke through his daydreams.

He sat upright, and groaned at what he saw.

The crowds were gathering nearby.

Eli's father had sent him with their family's boat to carry a rabbi and his students across the lake—to get away from these very crowds. Yet the people had guessed where the boat was going. They had walked around the northern end of the lake and were now fast approaching.

 Eli looked up the hill at the distant figures of the Rabbi and his students. They, too, must have seen the colorful array of approaching crowds, for the Rabbi was leading his students down to the shore to meet the masses of people who were gathering.

There were so many people that it took half an hour for all of them to get settled on the hillside. The Rabbi patiently allowed people to gather close about him. He stood at the base of the slope, with hundreds of people sitting in half circles that spread up the hill. His voice, carried with the breeze off the lake, reached them clearly.

Eli did not want any part of this. He knew his task was to stay with the anchored boat, just off shore, safely away from the large crowd. He saw no reason not to resume napping. So he leaned back again, intertwining his fingers behind his head as the curve of the boat supported him and closed his eyes.

But there was the man's voice . . . and his words.

Eli found himself listening carefully. Soon, he was sitting upright. This was no dry old rabbi, preaching in the way of the priests who burdened the people with hundreds of rules. This was no synagogue teacher lecturing until his audience squirmed. He did not speak of God or religion.

This man told stories. He made the people laugh. He engrossed them so deeply in what he was saying that they forgot their aching muscles, tired bones, and grumbling stomachs.

Eli, too, forgot about taking a nap. He forgot the lunch on the wooden seat beside him.

The hours passed, with Eli as spellbound as the crowd. Only when the sun began to nudge downward to the western hills did Eli realize this Rabbi had spoken the entire afternoon.

Only when the Rabbi finally stopped speaking did Eli see any restlessness in the crowd . . . or in the man's students.

Eli saw the Rabbi speak to one of the students, who spoke to another.

Then the apostles gathered to Jesus and told Him all things, both what they had done and what they had taught. . . . So they departed to a deserted place in the boat by themselves.

But the multitudes saw them departing, and many knew Him and ran there on foot from all the cities. . . . So He began to teach them many things. . . . When the day was far spent . . . He . . . said to them, "You give them something to eat.". . .

He said to them, "How many loaves do you have? Go and see."

And when they found out they said, "Five, and two fish."

And when He had taken the five loaves and the two fish, He looked up to heaven, blessed and broke the loaves, and gave them to His disciples to set before them, and the two fish He divided among them all. So they all ate and were filled. . . . Now those who had eaten the loaves were about five thousand men.

MARK 6:30, 33–44

Finally, one of the other students broke away from the group and walked down toward the boat.

Eli remembered this man, Andrew. During the journey across the lake, Andrew had talked with Eli of fishing, had talked like a man who knew about weather and water. Of course, Eli would remember this man, whose fingers, like all fishermen, were scarred with the deep cuts that came from handling heavy, wet nets.

But what could Andrew want from him?

"I see you have been listening to the Rabbi," Andrew said with a smile. "And what do you think of our teacher? Is he a man worth following?"

Eli nodded, suddenly shy to be treated like an equal.

"We are all hungry," Andrew continued. "And I happened to remember that you had some provisions with you. Do you have any left that you can share with us?"

Eli nodded again. In listening to the Rabbi, he had forgotten all about his lunch. He pointed at the bundle on the wooden seat—some small dry, barley rolls and the salty sardines he would use to flavor them.

"Please," Eli said. He did not think it would do more than whet their appetites, but he was glad to give what he could. "Take all I have. Five loaves and two fishes."

THE DEAF MAN

Hey!" Demetrius hissed to his friends. "Look ahead. There goes the idiot Donatus!"

Down the market street, beyond the heads of shoppers crowded between stalls, they saw the shoulders and back of a man carrying a basket of bread.

Demetrius, the leader of this band of twelve–year–olds, did not have to wave them forward. All of them, with Demetrius at the lead, broke into a run, weaving in and out of people on the street to catch Donatus. A deaf man, he was their prey as often as they could find him.

They stopped just a few feet behind him. Ignoring the stares and frowns of adults around them in the crowded market, they called to the man's back.

"Do you enjoy the taste of goat dung?" Demetrius asked loudly.

The pace of the man's walk remained the same. His shoulders did not flinch.

"If so," Demetrius chortled, "say nothing in reply."

Donatus said nothing, and the boys burst into laughter.

 Demetrius pushed locks of long, dark hair off his forehead, then cupped his hands around his mouth and howled at the man's back. The rest of his friends took their cues from him and danced behind the man, each of them howling with derision.

Donatus did not respond. He kept walking . . . his head held steady.

The boys doubled over with laughter.

A shopkeeper stepped out from behind a rack of of plucked chickens and spoke sternly to the boys. "Show some respect! We all know Donatus cannot help his affliction."

"You are right," Demetrius said, his face instantly sober. "You have our apologies."

The shopkeeper could not tell if Demetrius was mocking him. These boys had a reputation for mischief beyond belief.

Demetrius walked quickly in front of Donatus and put up a hand, gesturing with exaggerated politeness for him to stop.

 Donatus stopped, facing Demetrius squarely. He was a man of no great size, his hair speckled with gray. Nothing about his clothing distinguished him from any other laborer.

"Hello," Demetrius said to him. "How are you today? I am truly sorry if my behavior mocked you in any way."

Polite as the words were, Demetrius spoke with a slurring nasal tone, imitating the pitiful way the man spoke on the few occasions when he did so in public.

Behind the man, Demetrius' friends howled with laughter again. The shopkeeper shrugged and walked back to his stall.

"Yes, Donatus. Are you stupid?" Demetrius asked the deaf man in the same pathetic nasal mumbling. "Would you like to sit in a mud puddle?"

His friends egged him on from behind the man, choosing not to show themselves, for they considered it more amusing to remain an unknown audience to Donatus. The boy Demetrius continued for a few minutes until he could think of no other abusive things to say.

They brought to Him one who was deaf and had an impediment in his speech, and they begged Him to put His hand on him. And He took him aside from the multitude, and put His fingers in his ears, and He spat and touched his tongue. Then, looking up to heaven, He sighed, and said to him, "Ephphatha," that is, "Be opened."

Immediately his ears were opened, and the impediment of his tongue was loosed, and he spoke plainly.

MARK 7: 32-35

Finally, Donatus responded with a series of gestures. Demetrius translated for the benefit of his friends.

"You met a man today," Demetrius said, watching as the man first pointed to himself, then made walking movements with his fingers across his opposite palm. After a few more gestures, the man touched his fingers into his ears, then spit on his hand and rubbed it against his tongue.

"You plugged your ears and licked spit?" Demetrius asked, hardly able to keep a straight face. Of all the times he had mocked Donatus, this occasion was providing the most entertainment.

"No," Donatus answered quietly. "To save me embarrassment, the man kindly called me aside from the crowd. He put his fingers in my ears. He spit on his hand, and touched it against my tongue."

Demetrius almost fell backward in shock. The other boys—still huddled behind the man's back—exchanged incredulous looks. *Donatus had spoken normally!*

"His name is Jesus," Donatus continued clearly. "He comes from across the Sea of Galilee. There are others in our land whom he has healed also. Perhaps it would do you good to seek him out."

Demetrius backed away from Donatus. *Donatus had spoken normally! What insanity was this?*

"Furthermore," Donatus said, "if I hear any rude comments or howling from you or your friends again, I shall not restrain myself as I have today."

He took a threatening step toward Demetrius and laughed as the boy shot away. He turned and shooed the other boys, scattering them like chickens. He watched in satisfaction as they ran.

When Donatus resumed his patient walk, those around him heard something else they had never heard from him in all his years in the town.

Donatus was whistling . . . a cheerful tune!

HADORAM

Hadoram stood in the middle of a noisy, arguing crowd. The men around him saw the top of his head, his dirty tangled hair, the droop of his shoulders. What he saw of them were cloaks, purses hanging from waist belts, and sandaled feet. Somewhere, beyond the legs and feet of this crowd, Hadoram knew there was a big sky and a snowcapped mountain. He wished all the people would go away and leave him with the loneliness of the sky and wide open spaces.

 Noise and people disturbed Hadoram. He preferred to be quiet and alone, where he could sit with his arms around his knees and try to hold onto cool emptiness. Emptiness was good. When Hadoram heard noise, it was like a stick prodding sparks and ashes from the embers of the fire that burned inside him.

In his village, and especially in his home, he rarely found solitude. People in the streets spoke loudly, sometimes shouting, sometimes laughing. In his home, his baby sister cried and his mother argued with his father, often over Hadoram, their anger striking him like painful blows, because for Hadoram, anger in noise was worst of all.

Here in the middle of this crowd, away from the cool emptiness of the sky and horizon, among the noise and anger, Hadoram now felt the evil surge of that familiar growing fire. He could not explain this to anyone. There were times when he wanted the fire to go away, and water called him forth. There were other times when he loved the fire and wanted to embrace it, by joining with fire from wood. And then there were the terrible times when he wanted the relief of the water as badly as he wanted the fire to destroy him, and the two desires pulled at him and flung him from side to side like a monstrous lion shaking its prey until he fell to the ground and woke sometime later in a daze.

Anger and noise. Anger and noise. Here, in the crowd, surrounded by anger and noise, Hadoram was afraid this would become one of those times. Some force inside him could not help but greedily consume the anger growing around him.

"How can this Rabbi be the Messiah if his followers are useless?" This from a gray-bearded old man with a gleam of triumph stretched into a nasty smile.

"Useless? Hardly. He changed water into wine. He heals the lame with but a touch." This from one among a group of nine men facing the crowd.

"So you say," Graybeard cackled. "But all of you have laid hands on this boy and still the boy shudders. If your Rabbi has such great power, where is it among you?"

"It is a fever," one of the nine answered. "The father is wrong when he says a demon has hold of the boy. It is nothing more than fever."

 Someone else in the crowd grabbed Hadoram, roughly pushing his sleeve up his slim right arm, showing waxy ridges that drew gasps from onlookers. With the anger feeding upon him, Hadoram barely noticed he had been pulled into the center of attention.

"Does a fever leave scars like this?" the man said, shaking Hadoram's limp arm. "You can plainly see his flesh has been burned.

And look at the boy now. His eyes, rolling back in his head. This is no fever. So cast the demon away from him! Show us your power! Show us if your Rabbi is worth following. Or is he so afraid that he cannot show his face and leaves you to deal with this?"

Another man pulled Hadoram away.

"This is my son," the man said. "I came seeking the Rabbi to have him healed. Not to place him in the middle of your petty religious disputes."

 Love. Hadoram recognized his father's love beyond the fire inside, and he felt the rigidness of his body begin to ease . . . until his father dropped his hand and ran to the edge of the crowd, shouting something Hadoram could not understand in his swirling confusion.

Father. Where had his father gone?

The anger returned like a burning, suffocating cloak. Hadoram's breathing grew shallow again. Time did not move for him. Those around him watched him sway, with no sense of the battles raging inside him.

Then the crowd parted. People pushed Hadoram forward. He stumbled, uncertain of his surroundings, dimly aware that somewhere ahead was his father.

For a moment, as if a curtain had been pulled aside, Hadoram saw clearly, in a way he never had in those times when the furnace of anger consumed him. Beside his father, Hadoram saw a man—a man with such serene presence that it seemed a cool river of silent peace flowed outward from him.

In response, the anger within Hadoram roared, a sudden burst like a piercing thunderclap. Hadoram had never tried to resist the anger before, but now he wanted to reach for that river of peace. He tried to shout at the anger to let him go. He strained to touch even a finger in the river of peace from the calm man. But the anger held tighter. It became the monstrous lion again, shaking him and throwing him down, trapping his arms to his side with jaws of pain.

Time slowed.

Then more voices. Did Hadoram hear it with his ears? Or inside his head in the way that the anger sometimes spoke to him?

Lord, I believe. Help me in my unbelief . . .

. . . come out and never enter him again.

So much was happening. The fire of anger roared again, shook Hadoram again. Yet somewhere near was this wonderful river of peace, and he twisted and pulled against the invisible force, desperately seeking just a touch of that cool peace. And then . . . silence.

Hadoram found himself in empty silence. As if the ground did not exist beneath him.

More voices. In his head?

The boy is a corpse. The Rabbi killed him.

No, the voices were not in his head, but from the crowd.

Hadoram was in this world again, where he belonged. He no longer felt as if his lungs sucked at ash and smoke. Sweet breath filled him. He felt solid ground against his back and legs. He opened his eyes.

Above him was the sky and the mountain . . . and the man of love and peace reaching down to help him to his feet.

Hadoram smiled and took the man's hand.

It was the hand of his Savior.

When [the boy] saw [Jesus], immediately the spirit convulsed him, and he fell on the ground and wallowed, foaming at the mouth.

So [Jesus] asked his father, "How long has this been happening to him?"

And he said, "From childhood." . . .

Jesus said to him, "If you can believe, all things are possible to him who believes."

Immediately the father of the child cried out and said with tears, "Lord, I believe; help my unbelief!"

When Jesus saw that the people came running together, He rebuked the unclean spirit . . . and [the boy] became as one dead. . . . But Jesus took him by the hand and lifted him up, and he arose.

MARK 9:20–27

A FAMILY'S SALVATION

Zerah was almost round with fat. Though just eleven years old, his chin disappeared into his face and throat when he looked downward. His arms and legs bulged like stuffed sausages. And it did not help his appearance that he had inherited a distinct lack of height from his father.

Because he was the son of the household's master, the servants had no choice but to tolerate him as he waddled among them during meal preparation, tasting dishes and giving unwanted opinions and advice on food selection and choice of spices. Often, Zerah would steal large portions of food, forcing a servant to prepare a dish from the beginning again—the master also liked his food and did not tolerate shortages at the table.

Food was Zerah's pleasure, and it mattered little to him that he was fat. In the cloistered world of his life there were no others his age to taunt him. Not when he lived protected within the high walls that surrounded his father's mansion.

This meal's preparation began no differently from any other, with Zerah standing smugly among the servants, his dark greedy eyes darting from dish to dish, his fat lips already greasy from a snatched piece of roast lamb.

A commotion at the entrance, however, alerted the servants to a change of routine. They exchanged puzzled looks as laughter echoed with the arrival of noisy guests.

Guests? Laughter?

Zerah remained unconcerned.

His poked a finger in a cream sauce and licked it.

Not until his father called to him did he leave the servants and the food.

"Yes, father," he answered dutifully.

"Here are my friends," his father said. "I have invited them to dine with us this evening."

Zerah squinted suspiciously through pudgy eyelids. This was an ill-dressed bunch of rough-looking men, whose cheekbones were burned from endless hours in the sun. *Friends?* His father had no friends.

A man stepped forward from the others. He squatted, placed his hands on Zerah's shoulders, and looked directly into his eyes. For the first time ever, Zerah felt that someone had truly seen *him*—not his fat, not his shortness, not the heritage of hatred that came with being born the cursed son of Zacchaeus, the chief tax collector, but *him*—the boy with the lonely, aching heart.

 No words passed between the man and the boy, but Zerah felt a sure touch of love, a touch that awakened a long-buried loneliness, yet soothed that same loneliness with promised hope.

After the moment passed, the man stood, dropped his hands from Zerah's shoulders and moved past the boy as Zerah's father welcomed them deeper into the house, shouting with glee for his wife to join the celebrations.

That's all it had been from the man—a simple gaze, a simple touch.

Little as it was, it had been enough. Incredulous as the servants were after the guests' departure, Zerah understood when his father revealed that he had pledged half his wealth to the poor of Jericho.

The next day Zacchaeus took along his fat, young son as they ventured into the poorer streets, not to collect money but to distribute it. Zerah with his wheezing lungs and waddling legs could not endure more than an hour of walking his first day outside of their stately home. The next day, Zerah managed nearly two hours. And the day after that, three . . . and the day after that . . .

Then Zacchaeus stood and said to the Lord, "Look, Lord, I give half of my goods to the poor; and if I have taken anything from anyone by false accusation, I restore fourfold."

And Jesus said to him, "Today salvation has come to this house. "

LUKE 19:8-9

INTO HIS ARMS

After three years of ministry, Jesus is on a journey to death.

The final journey begins—as Mark describes it—in the north, on the brow of snow-capped Mount Hermon where Peter and James and John witness Jesus transfigured in glory.

It continues through Galilee, where Jesus tells his followers he is about to be delivered into the hands of men who will kill him. His followers are afraid to ask him more.

Jesus stops briefly in Capernaum, then moves into the hill country of Judea, the district across the Jordan River. Perhaps even as they cross the dark, slow-moving waters, Jesus remarks on the irony of a full circle, for this is the water where John first baptized him.

Soon—again as Mark describes it—Jesus and his disciples will begin the fifteen-mile journey on the road from Jericho to Jerusalem . . . where Jesus knows he will die.

While the disciples do not clearly understand the cross that lies ahead, through Jesus' tension they feel the chill of its shadow. To them, this is not a time for any man to be bothered by insignificant details . . . like women with children. Properly—to the disciples—this is a moment to protect Jesus from distractions.

Thus, when the women approach, the disciples see only bundles of inconvenience in their arms.

Jesus, of course, sees not an inconvenience, but children, hardly more than babies, small enough to take into the crook of his arm. Children with souls too young to have learned pride.

They also brought infants to Him that He might touch them; but when the disciples saw it, they rebuked them. Then Jesus called them to Him and said, "Let the little children come to Me, and do not forbid them; for of such is the Kingdom of God."

LUKE 18:15–16

Souls that are incapable of carrying a grudge or holding bitterness.

Souls so young, they trust without question.

Souls in need of protection.

Souls in need of a home.

He welcomes them into his arms. To Jesus they represent perfectly the kingdom of God, and he says as much to those around him.

And what do the children see?

Not the face of a faraway stranger, although he most certainly is.

Something about this man calms them. His smile, perhaps. The tone of his gentle words. His touch. Can it be that their innocent souls see the soul of this man of love?

 Although the cross looms for this man, they see nothing of that in his face. They are comforted, not alarmed. And when he moves on down the Jericho road he leaves them behind, blessed.

But who is not to say that these children in their small way have blessed him, too?

As he walks the road to the cross, perhaps the memory of these children, their innocence and need, give him, even in a small way, renewed strength and determination to face the pain and suffering and death that wait on a lonely hill outside Jerusalem. A death he accepts that we, too, might be welcomed into his arms.

TO SERVE A KING

To everyone in the village of Bethpage, Hilkiah's sullen look of perpetual disdain was a familiar sight. Perhaps it was because his parents had burdened him with the name of the famous high priest who had served King Josiah, the high priest who had found the book of the Law in the temple and, in so doing, had led Israel back to godly ways. Instead of trying to live up to his name, everyone agreed that the teenager Hilkiah seemed intent in every action on doing exactly the opposite.

Hilkiah's sullen disdain for life only worsened his appearance. His scraggly hair fell limp about his thin, shiny face, mottled with acne. Village gossip had it that this appearance was just punishment for his resentful attitude toward life. It did not occur to anyone that this sullenness and unkempt appearance might simply be a pretense of uncaring as defense against self-conscious adolescence.

On this Sunday, Hilkiah is loitering where he feels most comfortable, among the older teens and idlers of the village who are gathered in front of an inn at the crossroads. Jerusalem is across the valley, and hundreds of pilgrims are passing by each hour on their way to the Passover celebrations. These pilgrims provide ample fodder for insults—a sport enjoyed only by the idlers themselves.

 Two of these pilgrims have the audacity to untie a donkey colt in front of the inn. More amazingly, the colt's owner lets the pilgrims walk away with the animal, simply because they need it for a prophet named Jesus.

Hilkiah has heard vague rumors about this Jesus. He is a man, some

AN INNOCENT REBEL

Jesus' radical ministry of love managed to unite a diverse range of political opponents. Near the end of his third year of preaching and healing, it served all their best interests to see him dead.

To the Herodians, who favored Roman rule but wanted Herod to replace the governor, Jesus' growing earthly authority gave Herod less chance of gaining control of Judea.

As for the Pharisees, the teachers and interpreters of rabbinic law, Jesus not only insulted them publicly, he outright contradicted them, and gained such a following that people actually considered leaving the synagogues.

The Sadducees were the wealthy class of religious authorities who administered the temple and all the tithes that supported it.

claim, who can work miracles. What interests Hilkiah most is the fact that the Pharisees have issued notices that this man must be turned over to the authorities to be stoned to death. For Hilkiah, any person who rebels against the old graybeards is a person to rouse him from his usual sullen disdain.

When the prophet's followers pass in front of the inn, Hilkiah's curiosity draws him to join them. With a contemplative serenity, the prophet now rides the donkey, cushioned from the animal's spine by his followers' cloaks.

The small crowd of followers and close friends are also silent. Politically astute, they fear Jerusalem's reaction to Jesus' arrival. Despite the public postings for his capture, he has chosen to arrive in full view and open defiance of the temple authorities. The thought of his possible execution is sobering.

 Of most interest to young Hilkiah is the man someone identifies with a whisper as Lazarus, a man tall and vigorous in his strides—not the picture of someone they claim had been dead. *Did this Jesus actually call him forth from a tomb?*

Hilkiah remains with the procession as the road reaches a final crest before descending the Mount of Olives toward Jerusalem. It is here that the somber silence is broken.

Unexpectedly, a stream of pilgrims pours out from Jerusalem, rushing up the Mount of Olives. Word has reached them of Jesus' approach. They are loud, almost boisterous in their enthusiasm. They carry branches, torn from palm trees. As the colt bearing Jesus nears them, a few at the front of the crowd remove their cloaks and place them on the road. Others begin waving branches. Others shout for Lazarus to step forward, to prove he is alive.

By chasing the animals out of the market, Jesus disrupted their lucrative income. It was clear he was a threat to more than their religious beliefs.

On his final night, on trial in front of Caiaphas, Jesus faced a ruling body that drew from all three parties. It was no surprise, then, that this innocent rebel faced the death penalty.

Hilkiah is so surprised by these events that he forgets to be sullen. His shoulders lose their droop, and he raises his head as he watches all this with wide-eyed amazement. *Who is this prophet Jesus?*

Somewhere from the middle of the crowd come the first cries of praise.

"Hosanna! Blessed is he who comes in the name of the Lord! Hosanna!"

 Even Hilkiah, who avoids synagogue lessons, knows it is the welcome chant from the ancient psalms, often extended by people of Jerusalem to pilgrims. According to tradition, the pilgrims will respond within the second clause of each verse, and both parties will sing the last verse together.

This singing today is different from tradition, however. Much different. People point at Lazarus, whose miraculous rising from the dead has provided heated debate, speculation, and awe among the pilgrims visiting Jerusalem. Lazarus is the proof, they cry. Proof that all the other stories about Jesus must be true! Proof that a new Messiah has arrived to fulfill the ancient prophecies, a new Messiah with power to break the Roman oppression!

Around Hilkiah, the crowd fever grows and the hosannas become hoarse, broken utterances. From voice to voice, from soul to soul, the fire of unencumbered joy spreads.

Hilkiah, caught up for once in something greater than himself, joins in the shouts.

"Hosanna! Blessed is the King of Israel! Blessed is the coming kingdom of our father David! Hosanna!"

As the word spreads, it becomes a celebration, with thousands of people streaming out of Jerusalem to join the spontaneous parade.

Many of them are visitors to Jerusalem; some of them don't even know why they are dancing and singing with other strangers.

"Hosanna! Hosanna! Blessed is the King of Israel! Blessed is the coming kingdom of our father David! Hosanna! Hosanna!"

Hilkiah absorbs the joy, smiling and dancing with people nearby. The adults of his village would be astounded to see him now!

Suddenly a group of Pharisees pushes through the crowd. Hilkiah's sullenness instantly returns, for they remind him of his strict father.

These men are set apart by their religious caps and the tassels on their cloaks. Disgust is obvious on their faces. Disgust at the possibility of contaminating themselves by touching the common pilgrims. Disgust at the spectacle of these people worshiping a man the Pharisees hate.

The religious leaders begin to shout and strike people around them, and the hosannas cease. Complete silence falls, an eerie contrast to the frenzied shouting that had preceded it.

"Rebuke these people," the lead Pharisee commands Jesus with the full authority of a man accustomed to making people shrink simply by lifting an eyebrow. "You do not deserve this adulation. Call out now and send them away!"

Hilkiah, like others around him, holds his breath as the prophet stares at the Pharisees. No one, not even the wealthiest and most powerful, not even Herod himself, dares to defy the religious authorities openly.

Finally . . . long heartbeats later . . . Jesus points at rocks strewn along the edge of the road. He speaks slowly and clearly, so the crowd hears his restrained anger. "I tell you, if these people keep quiet, the very stones will cry out."

The Messiah has spoken! New shouts of acclamation drown out anything the Pharisees might say in reply.

Unbidden, the donkey colt moves forward. The prophet sways gently with its movement and ignores the Pharisees as he passes by.

Hilkiah's smile returns. A rebel at heart, he knows this man has a kindred spirit. Hilkiah decides to follow to learn more about him.

 Hilkiah does not know it yet, but what he will learn as he listens to Jesus in the temple over the next few days will transform his life, erasing his adolescent sullenness, motivating him to live up to the name given him at birth.

Yes, like his namesake, Hilkiah, too, will serve a king. But one far, far greater than Josiah—and he will serve not only for the rest of his life on earth . . . but for all eternity.

And it came to pass, when He drew near
to Bethphage and Bethany, at the mountain
called Olivet, that He sent two of His
disciples, saying, "Go into the village
opposite you, where as you enter you
will find a colt tied, on which no one
has ever sat. Loose it and bring it here.
And if anyone asks you, 'Why are you
loosing it?' thus you shall say to him,
'Because the Lord has need of it.'"

So those who were sent went their
way and found it just as He had said
to them. . . .

Then, as He was now drawing near the
descent of the Mount of Olives, the whole
multitude of the disciples began to rejoice
and praise God with a loud voice
for all the mighty works they had seen.

LUKE 19:28-32, 37

PALM SUNDAY

Now as He drew near, He saw
the city and wept over it.

LUKE 19:41

A girl and a boy—scruffy, dirty, lower class children whose parents had little concern for their whereabouts—dodged and twisted through the throng at one side of the road. The boy shot through a gap in front of a man on a donkey and stopped so quickly the girl almost fell on top of him. She lifted her hand to cuff him in playful vexation, but the sight that had mesmerized him stayed her hand. She, too, stared upward in awe.

It was the man on the donkey, riding beneath palm ranches held over him like a royal arch. His smile, which had first riveted the boy, was now cast upon the girl. He focused his entire attention upon them both with a gaze of such presence that a silence of instinctive, untroubled yearning covered them. So powerful was his smile that years later in occasional quiet moments the memory of it would soothe their souls with a caress as certain as a physical touch.

Followers behind the colt surged forward, and the moment passed as the crowd swept in front of the boy and girl, blocking their view of the man on the colt. Without exchanging words or glances, each turned to follow, trying to squeeze around the legs of the chanting adults. They stayed with the crowd as the road turned slightly downward, dipping out of sight of the corner of Jerusalem. The road rose again shortly, bringing the Holy City into full view for the first time.

What the children could not see, the man on the colt did.

Here, from the east, it seemed the city rose from a deep abyss—the valleys of Kedron and Hinnom. The temple tower dominated the

skyline, the vast temple courts spreading beneath. The monstrous temple walls on the eastern edge of the plateau seemed like cliffs—unassailable and as fixed as eternity. The upper palaces, brilliant white in the sunshine, now threw shadows across the garden terraces and the city below, giving an impression of unearthly splendor and an ache of beauty that could never fully be captured by memory or description.

What the children could not see, the man on the donkey did, as if in that single moment time's curtain rippled just enough to give him a ghastly vision . . .

> of earth heaped into ramps reaching the city walls,

> of legions of soldiers swarming triumphant,

> of a city outline marred by the smoke of destruction,

> of proud temple walls shattered into piles of rubble,

> of hundreds of rebels dying on crosses too numerous to comprehend,

> of wailing mothers searching the ruins for bodies of torn children—

> and then with another ripple of time, a new vision . . .

of dust swirling in an eerie dance to a dirge sung by the moaning wind as it blows across the desolation of centuries—the rejection by God himself in horrible, cold punishment for a city about to butcher his Son.

What the children could not see, the man on the donkey did—the beauty of the city and the inexorable tragedy ahead. The force of the contrast tore loose from him a wrenching sob so loud it startled those beside him. His sorrow deepened into heaving lamentation, spreading a pall of uneasy silence over his followers.

It was as if he spoke to the city when the agonized words left his mouth. "If only you had known on this day what would bring you peace—but now it is hidden from your eyes. The days will come upon you when your enemies will build an embankment against you and encircle you and hem you in on every side."

He closed his eyes, but could not shut out the vision overwhelming him. "They will dash you to the ground, you and the children within your walls. They will not leave one stone on another, because you did not recognize the time of God's coming to you."

His weeping did not stop.

 The boy and the girl crept forward. Unlike the adults, the terrible sorrow of the man on the donkey did not frighten them. It filled them with a longing to comfort him, as though he were a child in need of them. His sorrow drew them slowly to the colt where each shyly rested a hand on the hide of its flank.

For as long as he wept they walked wordlessly and shared his grief.

(from *The Carpenter's Cloth*)

THE MARCH
THROUGH BETHPAGE

Jesus' journey on Palm Sunday began in
Bethany, only a few miles from Jerusalem,
then moved through Bethpage, the town
where the disciples went ahead to find a
donkey colt, and on down the road to the
Temple in Jerusalem.

Bethpage lay on the eastern side of the
Mount of Olives, just below a summit that
gave view to Jerusalem. Some considered
Bethpage distinct from Jerusalem, for the
deep Kidron Valley separated it from the
city proper. Others—despite the valley
between—considered Bethpage an
extension of the city. During Passover and
the preceding days, the scattered collection
of buildings that made up the little hamlet
were filled to overflowing with festive
pilgrims who could not find room to stay
in Jerusalem.

At Passover time, little traffic followed the road away from Jerusalem. Instead, the road was jammed with devout pilgrims traveling toward the Holy City, coming in from Jericho and faraway places beyond. This collection of travelers—men, women, bickering mother-in-laws, mischievous children, camels, donkeys, and other stubborn beasts irritated by long days of travel—provided great amusement for the residents of Bethpage, who sat beside the walls of their homes and laughed at the boisterous, unruly parade.

WHAT THE HIGH PRIEST WORE

Thousands of priests served at the Temple. They all wore long white gowns tied with girdles, and white hats. Daily, each would rise before dawn to take a ritual bath. The clash of a gong thrown onto the pavement in front of the Temple called most of he priests to hours of ceremonial music and singing. The remainder of the priests would scatter for their usual duties—offering sacrifices for pilgrims at the altar in front of the Temple, lighting lamps, cleaning the altar of blood.

Of all the priests, one was in the supreme position, the high priest. He was the man with the greatest religious authority in the nation, and his dress reflected that authority.

A blue robe hung to his feet, covering all of his traditional, white priestly garmen ts except for the sleeves. From the bottom of the robe hung tassels with golden bells and pomegranates in alternation. Over the blue robe, he wore the ephod, a linen apron embroidered in bands of gold, purple, scarlet, and blue. A gold purse inset with twelve precious stones was a ttached to each shoulder of the ephod by a gold broach inset with sardonyx. On his head, the high priest wore a tall blue headdress banded with gold.

Dressed in this imposing manner, the high priest could force grown men to cower merely by lifting an eyebrow. How then, would an innocent child ever dare to approach him?

WHAT JESUS WORE

Along with his sandals, a typical Jewish man during the time of Jesus wore three or four articles of clothing—sometimes an innermost garment, then an under-dress, an upper cloak with girdle, and a head covering. As John reports in his Gospel, the soldiers at the Cross divided Jesus' clothing equally. Since the shoes, head covering, upper cloak, and girdle were roughly all of the same value, these four articles would have been easy to distribute without argument. But the expensive, seamless under-dress caused the soldiers difficulty because it was worth comparatively more than any of the other items, yet it would be worthless if ripped to pieces. They finally decided who could keep this inner garment by casting lots.

The head covering Jesus wore would have been a kerchief twisted into a turban. In Jewish culture it was considered a sign of disrespect to go without a head covering. Jesus' seamless inner garment—the under-dress—would have covered His body down to his feet. Any man or teacher who might publicly read or perform any duty in the synagogue absolutely had to show this modesty. This garment was secured around the middle of the body with a girdle, then covered with a square outer cloth that served as a cloak.

As a Jew, Jesus probably wore a cloak with tassels, which fulfilled the directives of Numbers 15:38–41 and Deuteronomy 22:12, serving as reminders to obey God's commands and be holy unto him. Yet given Jesus' teachings and attitudes toward the Pharisees, it is unlikely that he would have adorned his cloak with the greatly exaggerated fringes that they wore on their cloaks.

In contrast to the extravagant and intimidating appearance of the High Priest of Israel, children who approached such a humbly, comfortably dressed man as Jesus would feel safe and welcome.

THE CHILDREN'S HOSANNAS

Think of the children.

In the temple with their parents, there are babies in mothers' arms. Young boys, wriggling with energy, are bored by the seriousness they cannot understand. Girls, eyes wide with wonder, faces half hidden by wraps of cloth, sense already that much of the temple will always be barred to them simply because they are not male.

Then comes this man. A man of rage and action. A man who chases animals out of the market. A man who shouts. A man unstopped.

How could the children not be fascinated?

They see the reactions of their parents. Many parents applaud and cheer the man. Gone are the corrupt and hated thieves who extort money, who inspect animals and sell sacrifices at outrageous prices.

Some parents exchange stories. This is the prophet who raised Lazarus from the dead. Yes, the Pharisees have posted notices that he must be stoned. But listen, the Pharisees cannot stop him because of the crowds that follow.

Other parents, newly arrived in Jerusalem, are astonished, openly asking questions. Who is this man? Why haven't the temple police stopped him? Where is the man going now?

This man is followed, of course. By parents who cheer him, by parents who talk about him, by parents who speculate about him.

The children remain with their parents. So the children, too, are there in the courtyard. They see the miracles that take place on the steps of the temple.

This man touches a crippled beggar—and the beggar dances and sings.

This man speaks to a blind woman—and she weeps with joy, turning her eyes to family members she can finally see.

This man takes away groans and pain—he leaves behind peace.

The children look at the faces of their parents and see entranced wonder. The children look at the face of the man and see God-like love.

Around the children, some who were healed shout hosannas, echoing the welcome this man received as he rode a donkey colt into Jerusalem.

The children are touched by all this joy. They are simpler in heart and mind than their parents, closer to God in their innocence than the adults around them. They cannot help what their souls are called to do.

They burst into loud hosannas. Their sweet voices ring off the temple walls like a melody of angels gathered in a bouquet of praise.

Their hosannas interrupt the temple services, bringing forth stodgy old men with white beards resting on their chests. The old men shout with anger, demanding quiet.

This man in front of them sees through the hypocritical claims of these old men who declare that God must have reverence in his holy house, who demand that the children be silenced. This man admonishes the stern, outraged old men . . . and, to the children's amazement, the old men leave.

The children know. This man has great power.

The children continue to sing hosanna, for truth and love cannot be silenced.

This man Jesus smiles. It is reward enough.

(from *The Carpenter's Cloth*)

The blind and the lame came to Him in the temple, and He healed them. But when the chief priests and scribes saw the wonderful things that He did, and the children crying out in the temple and saying, "Hosanna to the Son of David!" they were indignant.

MATTHEW 21:14–15

THE BOY IN THE GARDEN

AN ILLEGAL TRIAL

Jesus' first trial took place in a great hall in the palace of Caiaphas, an area resembling an open court with an arched ceiling. As the trial began in the middle of the night, smoke from torches along the walls scorched the limestone with oily resin. The light, although dim, was strong enough to give shadowy outlines to the cracks of the flat, interlocked bricks that formed the floor, where rows of mats had been thrown down in three semi-circles to provide seats for the council members.

It was an illegal trial, for several reasons.

Rabbinic law dictated that such a case could only be tried in the regular meeting place in the temple. Furthermore, capital punishment could only be pronounced in the same place.

Also, according to rabbinic law, no process of trial was to begin at night or even in the afternoon. No trial could proceed on a Sabbath or on Feast Days.

On the night of betrayal, there is an unseen spectator in the garden of Gethsemane, a young man hardly more than a boy. He is there because he is curious.

At his father's house, barely an hour earlier, the boy had been sleeping soundly when Roman soldiers pounded on the door. He had listened from his bed as soldier's footsteps echoed through the house, squinted against lamp light from his bed as soldiers entered and briefly searched his room. The soldiers, led to this house by the disciple named Judas, were looking for the Rabbi Jesus.

The boy was acquainted with this Rabbi, for the boy had helped to prepare the upper room of the house for the Rabbi's Passover. The boy was also acquainted with Judas, for the boy had greeted all of the men who had entered the house just after sunset.

 But why, the boy asked himself, was Judas leading the soldiers and religious leaders back to the house? Why wasn't Judas with the Rabbi? The boy jumped from his bed, and hastily dressed himself, not bothering with undergarments in his rush to learn more. He stood still as voices carried up the stairs.

"There is only one place he can be at this hour," Judas told the soldiers, "in a garden where he often goes to be alone. It is called Gethsemane."

So, from a distance, shivering in the cold night, the boy followed the mob to the garden. He was confident no one would notice him.

Once there, his curiosity pays handsomely in what he is about to witness. Hidden in the shadows of the olive trees, he watches through the light of flickering torches as Judas steps forward to identify Jesus with a kiss. He sees Jesus step around the betrayer to challenge the soldiers with a question, "Who is it you want?"

"Jesus of Nazareth." The replying soldier speaks with bravado and contempt.

"I am he," Jesus says.

His calm, regal assurance is not only uncanny to the boy, but to the soldiers as well. This is not a man frightened by the full authority of the Roman empire, but one who acts as if he, not they, controls the situation. *A man . . . then . . . who might actually have performed the rumored miracles.* The soldiers' instinctively react with a superstitious fear of divine or magical retribution, and those closest to Jesus step back, stumbling on the feet of the soldiers behind them, so that more than a few trip and fall to the ground.

The boy fights an impulse to laugh, for swords and shields clank as the soldiers scramble to their feet. The rest of the mob has begun to press in, and there is no place for the soldiers to flee.

"Who is it you want?" Jesus asks again.

"Jesus of Nazareth." This time, the answer is respectful.

"I told you that I am he," Jesus says. He points at the disciples huddled behind him. "If you are looking for me, then let these men go."

 Lightning has not struck. Nor ghosts or demons appeared. The soldiers' fear passes, and Jesus' reminder of the other eleven men snaps the centurion out of a brief mental lapse. His military mind assesses possible danger.

Yet by the time the participants had assembled to pass verdict on Jesus, it was midnight on the Passover—a highly unusual and unprecedented occasion for a tribunal gathering.

Finally, in all capital cases, judges were expected to obey an elaborate system of warning and cautioning any witnesses. Not one judge was there to safeguard Jesus, the accused.

Thus, the men who worshipped the Law instead of God acted outside of that very same Law in their efforts to rid themselves of Jesus, his Son.

If the eleven men rush them, fighting will be difficult in the crowd. A Roman sword might strike one of the chief priests, and the political disaster from that would end his career.

"Now!" the centurion barks. Once they hold Jesus, the others will not dare attack. "Seize him!"

In the milling confusion of figures and shadows beneath flickering torchlights, the boy sees one of the Rabbi's followers move around the edge of the mob and surreptitiously withdraw a short sword from his clothing. It would be suicide to attack one of the armed soldiers and equally suicidal to injure anyone with the high political standing of high priest, so the man with the sword moves toward one of the servants.

"Lord!" The man shouts as he swings. "Should we strike them with our swords?"

His target jumps sideways at this warning cry, and the sword slices along his skull, shearing off part of his ear.

"No more of this!" Jesus commands. Although a soldier is about to grab Jesus, he steps away unhindered. No one stops Jesus as he reaches out to the whimpering servant.

 Jesus puts his left arm around the servant's slight shoulders to comfort him. With his right hand, Jesus touches the man's ear and when he pulls his hand away to examine it in the torchlight, he sees blood.

"Put your sword back in its place," he says to his follower, "for all who draw the sword will die by the sword."

The boy hears every word clearly.

"Do you not think I can call on my Father and he will put at my disposal more than twelve legions of angels?"

As calmly as Jesus has stepped away from the arresting soldiers, he returns to them. Because all attention is on Jesus, no one immediately notices the servant who is touching his ear in great wonder, amazed that the bleeding and pain have completely stopped.

No one except the boy, who will remember this night as long as he lives.

The appearance of resistance has been enough for the centurion. He commands the soldiers nearest him to form immediately behind Jesus.

Other soldiers move to capture the disciples, but they flee into the shadows of the trees, passing by the boy's hiding place. This draws a soldier's attention to the boy, who is caught by surprise in the soldier's strong hands.

The boy twists and turns frantically trying to escape. He spins away only by slipping through his outer garment and fleeing naked into the night.

The soldier chases after him.

"We have who we need!" barks the centurion. "Return and regroup!"

Thus, the boy escapes. But he does not flee too far. He has witnessed much and wants to see the end of all this.

He creeps back, retrieving his garment where the soldier had dropped it, and watches as the soldiers tighten a rope around Jesus' wrists.

Jesus looks over the soldiers at the chief priests and their servants. The boy hears him challenge them, unafraid.

"Am I leading a rebellion, that you have come with swords and clubs? Every day I was with you in the temple courts, and you did not lay a hand on me."

While He was still speaking, Judas, one of the twelve, with a great multitude with swords and clubs, came from the chief priests and the scribes and the elders. . . . They laid their hands on Him and took Him. . . .

Now a certain young man followed Him, having a linen cloth thrown around his naked body. And the young men laid hold of him, and he left the linen cloth and fled from them naked.

MARK 14:43–52

With all his soldiers around him, the centurion begins to lead Jesus back to Jerusalem. Jesus will remain silent for the entire journey, but he has last words for the chief priests.

"This is your hour," he says, "when darkness reigns."

 For the boy, it may well be the most important night of his life . . . a night of destiny. He will become a follower of Jesus, a helper to the apostle Paul. But that is not all. As a man this boy will later write down the complete story of Jesus' life from years of listening to the disciple Peter. But there will be one scene added by the boy's own unique witness. It is this scene in the garden that will forever endure in the Gospel named after the boy—the Gospel according to Mark.

THE YOUNGEST SOLDIER

GOLGOTHA

Golgotha, the hill of the skull, lay just to the north of Jerusalem. Near the main road, the crucified bodies gave adequate warning to any traveler who might be contemplating crimes against the Roman Empire.

It was not named, as many think, for skulls abandoned around the execution sites—Jewish law forbade the exposure of bones.

While there is some dispute over the exact site, many archeologists believe it is the hill that overlooks the Garden Tomb in Jerusalem. There, as anyone with the slightest imagination can see even today, the hill looks like a skull. It is a high, rounded rocky plateau like the dome of a man's head, worn by wind and rain to a dull gray. In the face of the hill, two shallow caves side by side, and a lower, larger cave centered below, form the two "eyes" and gaping "mouth" of a skull.

A deep purple sky, like an ominous thundercloud, covered the highest hills of Jerusalem. Occasional bolts of lightning, flashes of other-worldly yellow, outlined three crosses with gruesome burdens of dying men. An eerie, chilled calm swept the air, as if hail and lashing wind were about to whip the hilltop.

Yet the storm did not roll through. The clouds did not heave with expected and long-delayed violence. For nearly three hours, nothing dispelled the uncanny darkness and low rumblings of distant thunder.

Marcellus shivered. He told himself it was from cold. How long could it continue, this ghostly suspension of time?

He had wrapped himself in an outer cloak, his portion of clothing from the man hanging on the cross above him. The other three soldiers detailed to guard this cross had divided the man's headgear, his girdle, and his sandals, choosing to cast lots for his inner garment, a seamlessly woven linen.

All four soldiers had long since stopped mocking and toasting their captive with the cheap wine that Roman soldiers customarily brought to relieve the monotonous hours of crucifixion guard duty, waiting for exhaustion and dehydration to kill the victim of the cross.

Now each stood as still as the other, hiding fear, for darkness covered the sky as far as they could see.

Marcellus did not know the other soldiers well. There were twelve altogether—four for each of the three criminals, plus a centurion. He guessed, however, that the others, like him, drawn from the provinces to serve the Roman legion, were silently calling on their gods.

Earlier that bright spring morning, when they had escorted these men through the streets of Jerusalem, this had seemed like light duty. After all, with the Jewish Sabbath approaching, they would not be forced to remain at the execution site for days, supervising the usual lingering deaths. No, the bodies would need to be taken down by sunset, so all of them anticipated the breaking of legs to hasten suffocation, and a quick return to the barracks.

Yet at about the sixth hour, the sky had begun to grow dark. When the sunlight disappeared, their brave jesting quickly subdued to anxious waiting . . . and waiting . . . and waiting.

Marcellus did not know how much longer he could take the silence and the darkness. Sheer willpower held him in place, a refusal to be called a boy soldier by the older men who often teased him for his youth.

Seventeen years of age, red-haired, red-bearded, from the land of the Saxons, Marcellus had already spent two years serving his legion. During that time, he had seen friends die to the sword, had indeed slain men himself. All of it—forced marches, poor food, lack of sleep, the threat of sudden death—had made him stronger. He thought he was capable of facing any hardship or danger.

But this eerie darkness? The caves in the side of the hill only made it worse, black shadows emphasizing the face of a skull. Golgotha.

The darkness had muted the mournful cries of the women at the base of the cross. They were huddled together at the feet of a man they called the King of the Jews.

At certain times of the day, when the sun's light casts black shadows across these depressions, it is such a gaunt vision that any wind moaning across the barren stones seems to cry out with the groaning and cursing of all who have died tortured deaths within sight of those dead, dark eyes.

It was a curious crucifixion.

The King of the Jews. A worker of miracles, rejected by his own people. Was this of any significance? Surely the thick darkness was mere coincidence. Surely—

A croak from the man on the cross interrupted the young soldier's thoughts.

"Eloi, Eloi, lama sabachthani!"

Marcellus did not understand Aramaic, but someone nearby did.

"He calls for Elijah!"

Dimly, Marcellus saw outlines of movement. He tensed the grip on his spear. Was someone trying to free the man?

No, he realized moments later. Someone was placing a sponge on a stick and pushing it up to the dying man to drink.

Marcellus wished the darkness would end, that his edgy feeling of dread might be relieved by breaking clouds, by natural sunlight.

Another loud cry from the man on the cross—a death cry.

Then a horrendous boom of thunder, not of storm but of heaving earth, of granite breaking against granite, of grinding, splitting faces of rock.

Earthquake!

Marcellus dropped his spear and shield, fell to his knees, and braced against the shaking earth with both hands on the ground.

To his amazement, he heard his centurion cry out in fear! This was a grizzled veteran of war, a man missing two fingers on his left hand from a sword blow!

The horrendous thunder finally rumbled into silence.

And in that silence, his soul shaken with fear and awe, Marcellus listened to the incredible exclamation of the centurion—"Truly, this was the Son of God!"

Marcellus bowed his head and closed his eyes.

Days later those words still rang in his ears. Marcellus could not forget the death of that man. That's why he followed so closely the gossip in the soldier's barracks over the next days.

The religious leaders among the Jews still fear this man. They have requested that Pontius post a guard over the man's tomb. And, listen to this, Pontius actually agreed to their request . . .

When the news came on Sunday, those same gossiping soldiers sought out the young Marcellus.

"Did the man truly die?" they asked.

"Yes," Marcellus answered. He had seen the spear pierce the man's side, had seen the water and blood flow. Yes, beyond dispute, the man had died.

"Impossible!" they said. For now the tomb was empty. Despite the fact that the stone in front of the tomb was so heavy a man could not move it alone. Despite the fact that it had been guarded by Roman soldiers, soldiers who would face a penalty of death for failure in their duty.

And rumor was spreading. Not only among the soldiers but throughout the entire city. The man who had been crucified had been seen . . . walking and talking. He was alive!

How could this be?

Marcellus answered the only way he knew how. By repeating the words of the centurion.

"I saw him dead," Marcellus answered to the doubting soldiers, knowing it would be the first of many more times he would bear witness of that Friday afternoon, "so if he is now gone from the tomb, then truly this was the Son of God."

So when the centurion and those with him, who were guarding Jesus, saw the earthquake and the things that had happened, they feared greatly, saying, "Truly this was the Son of God!"

M A T T H E W 2 7 : 5 4

SELECTIVE BIBLIOGRAPHY

Alexander, Pat, ed., *The Lion Handbook to the Bible*. Oxford, England: Lion Publishing, 1973.

Barclay, William, *The Gospel of Mark*. Philadelphia: The Westminster Press, 1975.

Beers, V. Gilbert, *The Book of Life*. Elgin: Books for Living, Inc, 1980.

Connolly, Peter, *Living in the Time of Jesus of Nazareth*. Oxford, England: Oxford University Press, 1983.

Edersheim, Alfred, *The Life and Times of Jesus the Messiah*. Peabody, Massachusetts: Hendrickson Publishers, Inc, 1993.

Johnson, Luke Timothy, *The Real Jesus*. New York: HarperCollins Publishers, 1996.

Maier, Paul L., *Pontius Pilate*. Grand Rapids: Kregel, 1968.

Pixner, Bargil, O.S.B., *With Jesus Through Galilee According to the Fifth Gospel*. Rosh Pina, Israel: Corazin Publishing, 1992.

Pollock, John, *The Gospel of Mark*. Philadelphia: The Westminster Press, 1975.

Pritchard, James B., *Master, A Life of Jesus*. Wheaton: Victor Books, 1984.

Richman, Chaim, *The Holy Temple of Jerusalem*. Jerusalem, Israel: Cartam, The Israel Map and Publishing Company, 1997.

Ward, Kaari, ed., *Jesus and His Times*. Pleasantville: Reader's Digest General Books, 1987.

Wilkinson, John, *Jerusalem As Jesus Knew It*. London: Thames and Hudson, 1978.

Whiston, William, translator, *The Complete Works of Josephus*. Grand Rapids: Kregel Publications, 1960.

Yancey, Philip, *The Jesus I Never Knew*. Grand Rapids: Zondervan Publishing House, 1995.